P9-CCI-326

SOCIAL STUDIES ON THE INTERNET

SECOND EDITION

Michael J. Berson
University of South Florida

Bárbara C. Cruz
University of South Florida

James A. Duplass
University of South Florida

J. Howard Johnston
University of South Florida

PEARSON

Merrill
Prentice Hall

Upper Saddle River, New Jersey
Columbus, Ohio

Library of Congress Cataloging-in-Publication Data
Social studies on the Internet / Michael J. Berson . . . [et al.].—2nd ed.
p. cm.
ISBN 0-13-110808-5
1. Social sciences—Study and teaching—United States—Computer network
resources. 2. Internet in education—United States. I. Berson, Michael J.
LB1584.7.S63 2004
300´.285´4678—dc21

2002044491

Vice President and Executive Publisher: Jeffery W. Johnston
Editor: Linda Ashe Montgomery
Editorial Assistant: Laura Weaver
Production Editor: Mary M. Irvin
Production Coordination: Carlisle Publishers Services
Design Coordinator: Diane C. Lorenzo
Cover Designer: Harold Leber
Cover Image: Getty Images
Production Manager: Pamela D. Bennett
Director of Marketing: Ann Castel Davis
Marketing Manager: Darcy Betts Prybella
Marketing Coordinator: Tyra Poole

This book was set in Minion by Carlisle Communications, Ltd. It was printed
and bound by R. R. Donnelley & Sons Company. The cover was printed by Phoenix
Color Corp.

**Copyright © 2004, 2001 by Pearson Education, Inc., Upper Saddle River, New
Jersey 07458.** Pearson Prentice Hall. All rights reserved. Printed in the United
States of America. This publication is protected by Copyright and permission should
be obtained from the publisher prior to any prohibited reproduction, storage in a
retrieval system, or transmission in any form or by any means, electronic,
mechanical, photocopying, recording, or likewise. For information regarding
permission(s), write to: Rights and Permissions Department.

Pearson Prentice Hall[TM] is a trademark of Pearson Education, Inc.
Pearson® is a registered trademark of Pearson plc
Prentice Hall® is a registered trademark of Pearson Education, Inc.
Merrill® is a registered trademark of Pearson Education, Inc.

Pearson Education Ltd.
Pearson Education Singapore Pte. Ltd.
Pearson Education Canada, Ltd.
Pearson Education—Japan

Pearson Education Australia Pty. Limited
Pearson Education North Asia Ltd.
Pearson Educación de Mexico, S.A. de C.V.
Pearson Education Malaysia Pte. Ltd.

10 9 8 7 6 5 4 3 2 1
ISBN: 0-13-110808-5

For our families:

Ilene, Elisa, and Marc

Kevin, Cristina, and Amanda

Anne, Chris, Tina, Lizzie, Ellie

Lucinda, Christopher, Lisa, Kristin, and Dan

THE EASIEST WAY TO ENHANCE YOUR COURSE
Proven Journals • Proven Strategies • Proven Media

www.EducatorLearningCenter.com

Merrill Education is pleased to announce a new partnership with ASCD. The result of this partnership is a joint web site, www.EducatorLearningCenter.com, with recent articles and cutting-edge teaching strategies. The Educator Learning Center combines the resources of the Association for Supervision and Curriculum Development (ASCD) and Merrill Education. At www.EducatorLearningCenter.com you will find resources that will enhance your students' understanding of course topics and of current educational issues, in addition to being invaluable for further research.

How will Educator Learning Center help your students become better teachers?

- 600+ articles from the ASCD journal *Educational Leadership* discuss everyday issues faced by practicing teachers.

- Hundreds of lesson plans and teaching strategies are categorized by content area and age range.

- Excerpts from Merrill Education texts give your students insight on important topics of instructional methods, diverse populations, assessment, classroom management, technology, and refining practice.

- Case studies, classroom video, electronic tools, and computer simulations keep your students abreast of today's classrooms and current technologies.

- A direct link on the site to Research Navigator™, where your students will have access to many of the leading education journals as well as extensive content detailing the research process.

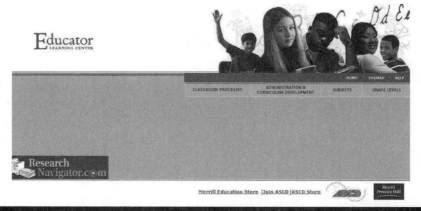

What's the cost?

A four-month subscription to Educator Learning Center is $25 but is **FREE** when used in conjunction with this text. To obtain free passcodes for your students, simply contact your local Merrill/Prentice Hall sales representative, and your representative will give you a special ISBN to give your bookstore when ordering your textbooks. To preview the value of this web site to you and your students, please go to www.EducatorLearningCenter.com and click on "Demo."

Preface

[This technology] is destined to revolutionize our educational system and . . . in a few years it will supplant largely, if not entirely, the use of textbooks.

Thomas Edison, 1922, statement on the invention of film

Claims of the importance of new technologies by the inventors are not limited to our current cultural advancements. Society's pundits have customarily proclaimed that advances in technology will reshape the face of the human experience. Historians point to the "Gutenberg revolution" as having reshaped the knowledge base, access to information, and learning process of Western civilization. Perhaps not as apparent, subsequent advances such as the chalkboard, ballpoint pen, mass production of paper, mimeograph machine, the public library system, overhead projector, radio, and television also have changed how we learn. The Internet might prove to be second only to the invention of written language itself in its significance as a learning process for society. Marshall McLuhan's declaration—that the problem today isn't that we don't have the answers, but that we don't have the questions—prophesied the new world of information created by the technology we call the Internet.

Social Studies on the Internet is an annotated collection of web sites for use by current and future teachers of social studies at the elementary, middle, and high school levels. It is a new doorway to the best practices, content, and original ideas that are essential to the success of social studies teachers. Mastery of the Internet and its resources can greatly enhance the quality of the learning experience in social studies classrooms.

In this second edition, every web site has been checked, updated, or replaced and new web sites have been added to reflect the developments on the Internet.

SELECTION OF SITES

In selecting the various web sites, four criteria were used:

1. *Comprehensiveness.* We generally selected web sites that offer the most comprehensive information and resources on topics of importance to social studies teachers.

2. *Durability.* It takes time, effort, and creativity to integrate the Internet into unit and lesson plans, and teachers need to have some reasonable assurance that their efforts will be usable in future years. Sponsoring organizations of national or regional reputation that serve as patrons of web sites will more likely provide the long-term stability and permanence that make it possible for teachers to put forth the effort to prepare lessons integrating technology.

3. *Self-Renewal.* We selected web sites that have a history of improvements and innovations to make the sites more usable, accurate, and up-to-date.

4. *Credibility.* Content on the Internet is fluid and without assurance that it is accurate. As is true of information in any medium, the source is a major consideration in evaluating its accuracy. The Internet has made it possible for content to be published in such an inexpensive manner that availability is no longer an adequate screening device. The volume of information in relation to the areas of expertise of reviewers has made it impossible for individuals to validate content. Therefore, emphasis was placed on sites whose patrons have reputations for service to the public good and are affiliated with well-respected organizations.

ORGANIZATION OF THE TEXT

The chapters in this text are organized as follows:

Chapter 1 is an introduction to the terminology of the Internet, various ways to use the Internet's resources, and sites that can provide a tutorial for novices.

Chapter 2 deals with Internet safety, legal and ethical issues regarding use of Internet material, and the integration of the Internet into social studies instruction.

Chapters 3 through 10 contain a wide range of social studies resources that social studies teachers at every level will find invaluable as they begin to use the Internet for their professional development, introduce the Internet into their classroom learning experiences, and change the way they teach. The web sites are organized into chapters based on content topics for ease of use by teachers when they prepare unit and lesson plans.

Chapters 11 and 12 offer social studies teachers a number of resources that will assist them on a variety of fronts, from planning and setting goals to accommodating diverse student populations.

Chapter 13 provides resources that will allow teachers to grow professionally and to respond to the classroom management challenges they face.

Within each social studies content chapter (Chapters 3 through 10), we have identified gateway sites, specialized sites, the kinds of information provided, and connections to NCSS themes. These identifiers will further assist you in determining the suitability of each site for your specific educational goals.

Sites

- *Gateway web sites* typically offer the most comprehensive access to information, multiple links to related web sites, and/or multiple applications (such as information, lessons, simulations, and virtual field trips). These gateway web sites appear first in each chapter or section of a chapter. Chapter 6's National Geographic web site, **http://www.nationalgeographic.com**, is an example of a gateway web site.

- *Specialized web sites* may also be comprehensive, but they are typically focused on a specific topic. Although less inclusive than gateway web sites, specialized web sites include the more focused collections of information or applications. The Betsy Ross home page at **http://www.ushistory.org/betsy** is one example of an elementary school-level site that is comprehensive, but on a limited topic. It is noteworthy that this web site is a link within a more comprehensive topic, Philadelphia Area Historical Sites at **http://www.ushistory.org**, which is sponsored by the Independence Hall Association. Because it is limited to the American revolutionary period, the Philadelphia Area Historical Sites web site would more likely appear as a specialized web site. These specialized web sites follow the gateway web sites in each chapter or section.

Application Icons

Each web site will have one or more of these icons in the *Icon Box* that appears in the margin, indicating the kind of information that can be found at the web site.

Icon	Title	Type of Information
	Asking Experts	An e-mail opportunity to communicate with experts
	Databases	A compilation of web sites or a searchable database from which information may be selected and gleaned
	E-Mail Pals	An e-mail opportunity to communicate with other students
	Elementary Emphasis	Resources that may be particularly appropriate for elementary social studies instruction
	Lesson Plans	Lessons developed by practitioners or curriculum writers
	Primary Sources	Original documents that can be downloaded and used in instruction
	Simulations	Active learning experiences
	Technical Assistance	Resources to improve learning
	Virtual Field Trips	Full-motion video or frames of a location
	Online Projects	Continuous, real-time projects

NCSS Themes

To further assist readers in curriculum or lesson planning, a quick reference *Guide Box* that includes the National Council for the Social Studies (NCSS) themes follows each web site.

The 10 NCSS themes have been adopted nationally as the core of social studies instruction:

I   Culture

II   Time, Continuity, and Change

III   People, Places, and Environments

IV   Individual Development and Identity

V   Individuals, Groups, and Institutions

VI   Power, Authority, and Governance

VII   Production, Distribution, and Consumption

VIII   Science, Technology, and Society

IX   Global Connections

X   Civic Ideals and Practices

A full explanation of the themes appears on the NCSS web site at **http://www.ncss.org/standards**. One or more of these Roman numerals in the *Guide Box* indicates that the web site has excellent potential to support instruction to achieve the indicated standard(s).

We believe these sites will prove to be valuable to teachers of social studies as we strive to improve the quality of social studies education for the next generation of citizens in our country and the world.

ACKNOWLEDGMENTS

We wish to acknowledge the assistance of the following individuals: Ilene R. Berson, Aimee Fogelman, Shelli Whitworth, Ursula White, and students in Social Science Education courses at the University of South Florida.

We would also like to thank the reviewers of our manuscript for their insights and comments: Bruce E. Larson, Western Washington University; Jay A. Monson, Utah State University; Tom Savage, California State University, Fullerton; and James J. Zarrillo, California State University, Hayward.

Michael J. Berson
Bárbara C. Cruz
James A. Duplass
J. Howard Johnston

Contents

Note: Every effort has been made to provide accurate and current Internet information in this book. However, the Internet and information posted on it are constantly changing, so it is inevitable that some of the Internet addresses listed in this textbook will change.

CHAPTER 1

Internet Basics

The **Internet** is a global arrangement of networks made up of millions of individual computers. Its primary capability is known as the **World Wide Web (WWW or web).** The U.S. Department of Defense laid the foundation of the Internet over 30 years ago with ARPANET. In 1993, there were approximately 130 web sites; now there are millions, **http://www.isoc.org/internet/history/brief.shtml.**

To organize the information on the World Wide Web, **Uniform Resource Locators (URLs)** were created to provide site addresses (an example would be **http://www.NCSS.org**) so that you can use a **browser** to move from one web site to another. Example 1-1 shows Social Studies Online of the National Council for the Social Studies (NCSS) as presented by the Netscape browser. This first Social Studies Online view is referred to as a **home page** or **web page;** its URL is **http://www.socialstudies.org**. Browsers like Netscape, Microsoft's Internet Explorer, and Mosaic can be used to find and access this and other URLs.

If you know the address of a site that you want to visit, you can type the address in the "Location" box at the top part of the browser (see Example 1-1) and press the **"Enter"** key. The software will process the request and take you to the web site. You must type the address exactly, or you will receive a message indicating that the location cannot be found. Addresses can change from time to time, but often the old address will point you to the new address. Also, you should be aware that names can be misleading. Whitehouse.gov is the White House of the United States of America; Whitehouse.com is a pornography gateway site.

INTERNET ORGANIZATION ADDRESSES

Most people are familiar with the first part of the Internet address, which appears before the colon. This identifies the type of resource or method of access. For example, **http** stands for a hypertext document or directory. Less familiar, but valid sources are **gopher, ftp, news, telnet, WAIS,** and **file.**

The second part of the address is usually the address of the computer where the data or service is located—typically, the home page. Additional parts may specify the name of a file, the port, or the text to search for in a database. The National Council for the Social Studies uses **"social studies"** to identify the home page in Example 1-1.

Example 1-1   A Home Page: www.socialstudies.org

Reprinted with permission of the National Council for the Social Studies.

Domains classify broad types of providers based on their mission and are typically indicated by two or three letters. NCSS is an "org," for organization. Table 1-1 is a list of common domains.

BROWSERS AND SEARCH ENGINES

When you enter the web, the first page you see is the **browser** page (see Example 1-2).

If you do not know the address of a web site, the tool you can use to find information is a **search engine.** Example 1-2 includes several search engines, with the **About.com** search engine highlighted. Search engines such as **About.com, Excite, Lycos,** and **Yahoo** work in conjunction with browsers.

SEARCHING THE INTERNET

If you do not know a site's address, but have a name like George Washington, NCSS, or National Council for the Social Studies, you can enter that information in the **search box** (under "Search the Web" in Example 1-2) of the search engine, and it will return a new image listing possible sites that match the words you typed in the search box. No two search engines give the same results because they

Table 1-1   Domains

Domain	Type	Example	Source
.com	Commercial organization	dell.com	Dell Computer Corporation
.edu	Educational institution	usf.edu	University of South Florida
.gov	Government organization	lcweb.loc.gov	Library of Congress
.int	International organization	nato.int	NATO
.mil	Military site	monmouth.army.mil	Ft. Monmouth Army site
.net	Network organization	promo.net/drnet	Ask Dr. Internet
.org	Professional organization	NCSS.org	National Council for the Social Studies
.uk	Country	aaranet.co.uk	Aaranet is a network service in the United Kingdom

have different protocols for harvesting web site locations. These listings of possible sites are known as **hits.** You can also use search engines to search for topics. You simply type in a word or phrase like "Ben Franklin," "De La Salle High School," "lesson plans," or "Renaissance." Once the search engine provides you the list of hits, you can click on any one of the items, and the search engine will take you to the web site.

You can efficiently search the Internet by paying attention to a few simple rules. If you type *George Washington* into the About.com search engine, you will get over 500,000 hits because About.com will list all sites mentioning george or washington. If you add quotes (*"George Washington"*), you get over 100,000. If you type *"George Washington" and "Mount Vernon"* you produce 130,000 hits. But if you type the *and* as AND, the search is narrowed, and you produce about 3,700 hits. The most common and useful **operators** for searching are **AND, OR,** and **NOT.**

TROUBLESHOOTING

You may find that a given web site's address has been changed. Often, you will automatically be transferred to the new site. If this does not occur, you may try deleting any words or letters after the extension (e.g., the ".com" or ".edu"). Another strategy is to type in the name of the site in quotation marks in a search engine such as AltaVista or Yahoo.

Example 1-2   Browsers and Search Engines

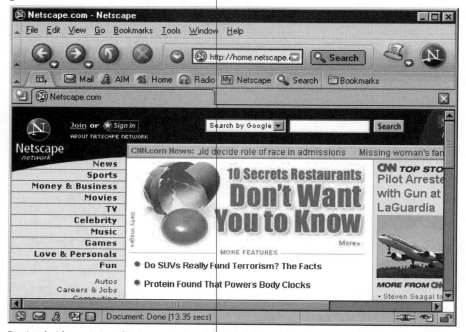

Reprinted with permission of Netscape: Portions Copyright Netscape Communications Corporation, 1988. All Rights Reserved. Netscape, Netscape Navigator, and the Netscape N Logo are registered trademarks of Netscape in the United States and other countries.

Reprinted by permission. Infoseek, Ultrasmart, Ultraseek, Ultraseek Server, Infoseek Desktop, Infoseek Ultra, iSeek, Quickseek, Imageseek, Ultrashop, the infoseek logo, and the tagline "Once you know, you know," are trademarks of Infoseek Corporation which may be registered in certain jurisdictions. Other trademarks shown are trademarks of their respective owners.

WEB SITE ORGANIZATION

There are four basic types of web site organization:

1. A page of information, as in Example 1-3, that you can scroll through to locate the exact information you are seeking.

2. A home page with **internal links** to pages within the web site that are authored and controlled by the organization. Example 1-1 from the NCSS reveals internal links, but it also includes the heading Internet Resources and Links.

3. A home page with **internal links** to pages within the web site that are authored and controlled by the organization and with **external links** to other web sites that are authored and controlled by other organizations. In some cases, one cannot tell which links are internal and external because they are not grouped as NCSS has done.

Example 1-3   Search Engine Hits

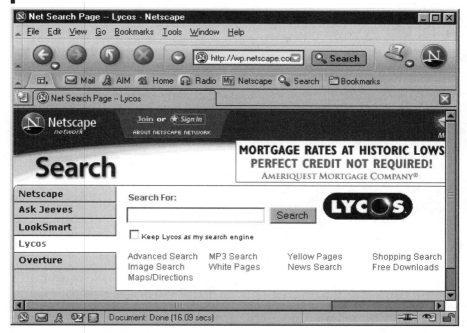

Reprinted with permission of Netscape.

4. A home page with only **external links** (see Example 1-4) to other web sites that are controlled and authored by other organizations.

To navigate through the links, you typically point and click on a link with your mouse. Example 1-4 depicts two typical types of "clickable" links. Once you are transferred to the link you clicked on, the address displayed in the "Location" box of the browser will indicate if it is an internal or external link. This distinction is important to social studies educators because decisions about the accuracy and credibility of information are in part dependent on its source.

BOOKMARKS

Keeping track of your web sites with your **Bookmark** or **Favorites** tool can mean significant savings for you in terms of time and keyboarding strokes. When you find a useful web site, click on **Bookmark** at the top of the screen, and add it to your collection. As you harvest more and more valuable sites, you can then group your bookmarks into meaningful folders such as U.S. History, Geography, and Current Events.

| Example 1-4   Links

     WWW-VL History: Central Catalogue

WWW-VL Central Catalogue
WWW-VL Search Facility

Important Information
About This Network
To Send Comments and Suggestions
To Recommend a Site

Research: Methods and Materials
Finding Aids: Bibliography - Guides - Indexes -
Libraries - Archives - Manuscripts - Museums -
Booksellers
Materials: Electronic Texts - Historical Journals - Data
Bases - General Reference Works - On-Line Images -
Maps for Historians
Methods and Auxiliary Disciplines: - Methodologies
- Archaeology - Demography - Genealogy - Language
- Timelines
Instruction: Instructional Resources - Distance
Education - Employment - Grants - Information Quality

By Countries and Regions

Africa: African Studies - Algeria - Djibouti - Egypt -
Liberia - Libya - Mauretania - Morocco - Somalia -
South Africa - Sudan - Tunisia

Americas:
- Argentina - Belize - Bolivia - Brazil - Canada - Chile -
Cuba - Ecuador - Guatemala - Honduras - Mexico -
Peru - United States

Asia:
West: Armenia - Azerbaijan - Bahrain - Comoros -
Georgia Iran - Iraq - Israel - Jordan - Kuwait - Lebanon
- Oman - Palestine - Qatar - Saudi Arabia - Syria -
Turkey - Tunisia - United Arab Emirates - Yemen
Central: Afghanistan - Eastern Turkistan -

Reprinted with permission of Lynn H. Nelson.

LEARNING MORE ABOUT THE INTERNET

If you would like to learn more about the Internet, the Library of Congress offers a
gateway to a broad range of information about the Internet:
http://lcweb2.loc.gov/learn/resources/inres/gen/using.html

At Webteacher, there is a tutorial on the Internet designed with teachers in mind.
http://www.webteacher.org/windows.html

But ultimately, the best way to learn the Internet is to explore. The following
chapters offer a wide range of social studies and education-related web sites that
provide points of departure into World Wide Web resources that will make a
difference in the classroom experience of your students.

CHAPTER 2

Before You Begin

The Internet is a tremendous resource for schools that facilitates research, education, communication, and entertainment. Moreover, it is a tool that is being accessed with increased frequency. The U.S. Department of Education reported in 2001 that approximately 98 percent of schools have the capacity to support online initiatives. In the very near future U.S. schools will have achieved universal access.

Although the online world offers many enriching opportunities for students, its expansive and global context still contains risks and potential dangers. Recognition of its disadvantages is necessary for making choices and managing risks with creative and common sense solutions that promote protective and productive learning environments for children.

Although some of the Internet problems for schools are extensions of the common issues faced by parents when children access the Internet from home, schools also have unique issues that are specific to the educational setting. Common risks include potential interactions with cyberpredators who lure children to face-to-face encounters; exposure to content and information that is inappropriate for children, including pornography, violence, hate, misinformation, and hoaxes; access to products and information that may be used to harm them or others, such as guns, drugs, alcohol, and bomb-building recipes; harassment online with threats, insults, and the transmission of viruses; invasions of privacy and subsequent targeting for unfair marketing strategies; and scamming and defrauding through disclosure of financial information, such as credit card numbers and passwords. Schools also must address issues such as use of students' photos and personal information on school web sites, plagiarism of Internet resources by students, student access to nonschool sites, the restriction of speech when online, students' skills in assessing the credibility of online resources, and informed consent of parents for their children's online activities at school.

Safety on the Internet depends on the education of administrators, teachers, parents, and students regarding procedures to promote well-being and minimize risk. Whether a child is just learning how to use a computer at school or is an experienced user of technology, educators have an opportunity to enhance children's safety before they become avid explorers of the wonders of cyberspace. By taking responsibility for children's online computer use, adults can greatly minimize potential risks and assist children in experiencing the exciting global resources of the Internet.

The following guidelines are designed to create boundaries and barriers that promote safety:

1. The best way to assure that young people are having positive online experiences is to supervise their activities. Monitor students' computer activities by placing the computer in an easily viewable area. Maintain open communication about information they have found, sites they have explored, and people with whom they have chatted.

2. Investigate the use of filtering software. But even with these controls, you still need to be involved. An excellent resource regarding filters can be found at: http://netizen.uoregon.edu/Constitutionality.pdf.

3. Establish an acceptable use policy for the Internet. Childnet International has developed a special "Children's Bill of Rights for the Internet" (http://www. childnet-int.org/resources/billofrights.html). The GetNetWise project (http://www. getnetwise.org/safetyguide/tips/kids.php) has created a site that outlines suggested children's rules for online safety. These include basic rules, such as:

   a. Never give out identifying information (i.e., Full Name, Home Address, Telephone Number, Age, Race, Family Income, School Name or Location, or Friends' Names) online unless your parents have given you specific permission. Be sure that you are dealing with someone that you and your parent/guardian know and trust before giving out any personal information. Also, remember that online information is not necessarily private.

   b. Never send a picture or video of yourself to another person without the permission of your parent or guardian.

   c. When someone offers you gifts, money, or other offers of "something for nothing," tell your parent, guardian, or teacher.

   d. Tell your parent, guardian, teacher, or other trusted adult if you come across any information that makes you feel uncomfortable or confused. You should be especially cautious if messages imply secrecy or describe mechanisms for hiding information from parents, teachers, or other supervising adults. Do not respond to these messages and end the communication immediately.

   e. Never arrange a face-to-face meeting unless your parent or guardian gives permission. If you have parental consent, make sure that you have a parent or guardian with you and arrange to meet in a public place.

   f. Remember that people online may not be who they say they are. Because you can't see or hear the person, it is easy to pretend to be someone else.

   g. Never use rude language or send mean messages. Treat other online users with respect.

   h. Do not give out credit card information without your parent's/guardian's permission.

   i. Never share your password, even with friends. When sites request a password, pick a different one than your log-on code.

The Internet can also be used by educators to assist them in understanding online risks and establishing rules and guidelines for safe web exploration by students. The following sites are a few links that will be helpful in this important area of promoting children's safety.

The CyberSmart! Curriculum

http://www.cybersmart.org/home/

The CyberSmart! Curriculum provides a comprehensive training for students K–8 which empowers them to use the Internet safely and responsibly. The curriculum includes 65 lessons that are correlated to the National Educational Technology Standards. Students acquire skills in safety, explore manners and responsible Internet use, focus on advertising and privacy online, examine the use of online resources for research, and reflect on technology in the past, present, and future. This valuable teaching resource can be downloaded free of charge from the web site, and teachers or school districts can arrange for staff training on implementation of the curriculum through web-based, self-paced courses that are offered at reasonable prices and with continuing education and college credit available.

iTECH Inc: School Acceptable Use Policy Links

http://www.aupaction.com/aupsonweb.html

This site provides useful links to school acceptable use policies that may assist educators in developing and reevaluating their current communication of guidelines to parents and students for online access in school.

National Center for Missing and Exploited Children (1-800-The Lost)

http://www.missingkids.com/cybertip

This private, nonprofit organization provides assistance to families of missing children and conducts prevention and awareness programs. A CyberTipline has been created in collaboration with the Federal Bureau of Investigation (FBI), U.S. Postal Service, and Office of Juvenile Justice. When you come across child pornography on the web, you should report it by calling or contacting the above site.

National Institute for Consumer Education

http://www.emich.edu/public/coe/nice/fraudml.html

The National Institute for Consumer Education has prepared this mini-lesson plan to help students identify and describe examples of Internet fraud and list ways to protect themselves from it.

Safe Kids Online

http://www.safekids.com/

This site allows access to the full text of Larry Magid's popular child safety and teen safety brochures.

NetSafe

http://www.netsafe.org.nz

The web site of the Internet Safety Group of New Zealand offers information on various aspects of safety on the net.

LEGAL AND ETHICAL ISSUES IN CYBERSPACE

The study of law and ethics facilitates an understanding of guidelines that direct our conduct and maintain the cohesiveness of our society. Thoughtful consideration of belief systems that contribute to the formulation of laws and policies can contribute to critical dialogue on morals, values, and constitutional liberties. The following web sites present a full range of contemporary legal and ethical issues that may aid in instruction on responsible behavior, individual rights, and the process of decision making when confronting dilemmas.

Responsible Netizen

http://responsiblenetizen.org/

The Responsible Netizen site provides extensive information on young people's safe and responsible use of the Internet. The site includes access to online documents and publications that address emerging issues on legal decisions and efforts to promote ethical behavior in cyberspace.

University of British Columbia, Center for Applied Ethics

http://www.ethics.ubc.ca/resources/

The Center for Applied Ethics at the University of British Columbia provides an opportunity for academics, ethicists, and others to engage in research and reflection on contemporary moral issues. The site links readers to applied ethics resources on the web, including working papers, discussion groups, codes of conduct, various newsletters, ethics courses, and search engines. The user is presented with 15 subcategories relating to applied ethics. The Computer and Information Technology icon connects readers to organizations, publications, and legislation. Some topics covered are censorship, intellectual property rights, teaching and technology, and socioeconomic issues relating to the Internet; other icons offer information relating to ethical use of the Internet. These include Science and Technology, Media, Health

Care, and Business. The center has established an electronic clearinghouse that serves as a reliable and accurate filter for issues concerning ethics and cyberspace.

Electronic Privacy Information Center (EPIC)

http://www.epic.org/

EPIC, located in Washington, D.C., describes itself as "a public interest research center" designed to alert the public to privacy and other civil liberty issues. It is a project of the Fund for Constitutional Government and works in association with other human rights groups. This site provides current news on policies affecting privacy and other constitutional privileges. Visitors can also view government documents obtained by EPIC through the use of the Freedom of Information Act.

Center for Democracy and Technology

http://www.cdt.org

This site provides visitors with a guide to pending federal legislation regarding issues such as free speech, data privacy, and cryptography. This nonprofit public interest organization claims to advance "democratic values and constitutional liberties in the digital age." Links to other resources, including state, national, and international organizations and government agencies, are also provided.

H-Net Citation Guide

http://www.h-net.msu.edu/about/citation/

H-Net is designed to advance teaching and research in the arts, humanities, and social sciences by providing an open forum for the exchange of ideas and resources among educators. The main feature of this site is the topical discussion newsletters,

Reprinted with Permission of Michigan
State University/H-Net Humanities Online

or "lists," that provide visitors the opportunity to share ideas on the topic provided. These interactive lists lead to discussion threads, important documents on the topic, related classroom activities, and links to other sites. The discussion lists also provide information on job postings, fellowship opportunities, and upcoming conferences in particular areas. H-Net also provides training to scholars on advancements in the areas of computing and electronic communication in order to promote the use of technology in the classroom. This site also provides visitors with gateways to multimedia teaching centers, syllabi in the area of interest, conference papers, and web-based teaching projects. Finally, H-Net presents scholars with the opportunity to create their own discussion networks.

Additional Cybersafety Sites

Center for Media Education
http://www.cme.org

Computer Learning Foundation
http://www.computerlearning.org

Cyber-Plagiarism
http://tlt.its.psu.edu/suggestions/cyberplag/

U.S. Department of Justice
http://www.usdoj.gov/kidspage

Sophos Anti-Virus Information
http://www.sophos.com/virusinfo/

Urban Legends Reference Page
http://www.snopes2.com/

Canada's Media Awareness Network Cyber Pigs
http://www.media-awareness.ca/eng/cpigs/cpigs.htm

Information Literacy Primer
http://glef.org/tiliteracy.html

KidSmart
http://www.kidsmart.org.uk/

Surf Swell Island

http://www.surfswellisland.com

U.S. Department of Education Internet Safety

http://www.ed.gov/Technology/safety.html

Childnet International

http://www.childnet-int.org/

Kidz Privacy

http://www.ftc.gov/bcp/conline/edcams/kidzprivacy/index.html

INTEGRATING THE WEB INTO SOCIAL STUDIES

For the constantly changing subject area of the social studies, the World Wide Web offers a vast array of learning opportunities. Some of the more notable are:

- using the WWW as a research tool;
- promoting active learning;
- developing critical thinking and problem-solving skills;
- enhancing cooperative and teamwork skills;
- obtaining primary documents and facsimile artifacts;
- establishing e-pal correspondence exchanges;
- telecommunicating and teleconferencing;

◼ providing visuals for topics and places studied; and

◼ Aiding teacher preparation (e.g., background research, pedagogical strategies, lesson plans).

The following sites provide valuable initial direction in the integration of the WWW into your social studies classroom.

Coalition for Innovation in Teacher Education (CITE)

http://www.teacherlink.org/content/social/

The Coalition for Innovation in Teacher Education (CITE) at the Center for Technology and Teacher Education at the University of Virginia, has created a social sciences forum for educators at the K–12 and university levels.

The Instructional Resources section of this site is a collection of lessons that combine social science instruction and technology. These lessons are separated into two categories: Modules and Web Resources. Modules are specific lesson plans that provide educators with objectives, materials needed, procedures, assessment, and related resources for subject matter such as the Declaration of Independence, the Marshall Plan, and a White Southerner's Defense of Slavery.

The other component of The Instructional Resources section is the Web Resources feature. It contains exemplary web resources that have been selected and categorized by members of CITE. These resources are organized into the following categories: Professional Resources, Teaching Resources, Telecollaborative Projects, Reference Materials, Archives, and Digital Resource Centers.

The Professional Resources component contains web pages that are specifically developed to assist social studies teachers in the classroom. This feature provides lesson plans and links to other notable social science web pages. Some examples of these resources are Gateway to World History, Awesome Library K–12 lesson plans, and American Memory Learning Page.

Teaching Resources is a collection of web pages containing subject matter that can be incorporated in the classroom to guide individual student or whole class instruction. Examples of these web pages are Renaissance, Pilgrim Life, and Africans in America.

The Telecollaborative Projects component provides a collection of web pages designed to promote collaborative projects among social studies students and teachers around the globe. It has links to classrooms that allow teachers to design and share classroom Internet projects. Some examples of these projects are Ask Thomas Jefferson, Geo-Mystery Project, and Email around the World.

Reference Materials is a web resource similar to a reference section in the library. It has web pages designed to allow students and teachers to access up-to-date information. Some examples of these helpful reference materials are *CIA World Fact Book*, *Libraries around the World*, and *Old Farmers Almanac*.

The Archives component of the Web Resources feature is a collection of web pages that have authentic data that students can research and reference for assignments. Some examples of these archives are the Vatican library, U.S. Census

Bureau, and *Penny Magazine*. Teachers may also find this an invaluable resource for activities by finding actual documents that support their subject matter.

The Digital Resource Centers component allows users to locate exemplary digital resource centers and explore other instructional ideas. For example, educators can click on Digital Media Center, Geospatial and Statistical Data Center, and Center for Electronic Texts in the Humanities to explore ideas for including technology resources into their curriculum.

The next section of the social sciences forum is Software Reviews. This is a database that has noteworthy social studies software titles and reviews. Visitors can browse for products of interest by viewing product titles, which are separated by subject matter, grade level, and type of activities. This resource also contains reviews of available educational software and allows teachers to submit their own review of software by using a CITE evaluation form.

The social sciences forum also contains a useful resource in the Case Studies section. This provides visitors with case studies that can be used in a social studies method course to engage preservice teachers in reflecting upon the possibilities of technology-based instruction in classrooms. For example, one case study illustrates how a teacher used technology to investigate essential freedoms through the Bill of Rights, and another case study presents a teacher using technology to help students with reports on different countries.

Another helpful section in the social science forum is the Digital Resource Centers. This feature allows users to locate exemplary digital resource centers and explore instructional ideas. One of the resource centers, for example, is the Perseus Digital Library, which has hundreds of Greek and Roman resources in art and in archaeology and an interactive atlas of the classical world. This section is very helpful because it contains many relevant transcriptions of historical letters, texts, diaries, poetry, and prose. Teachers can access some of the actual documents that may be used to illustrate the culture of certain eras.

The final section of the social sciences forum created by CITE is the Discussion Groups. This feature provides users with access to CITE discussion groups that promote conversations with others interested in similar topics. Educators can then share ideas and get helpful feedback in order to expand their vision and use of technology in the classroom.

Additional Sites for Integrating the Web

Kathy Schrock's Guide for Educators: Critical Evaluation

http://school.discovery.com/schrockguide/eval.html

Hobbes' Internet Timeline

http://www.zakon.org/robert/internet/timeline/

CHAPTER 3

United States History and Cultures

United States history involves an exploration of facts concerned with American phenomena that have taken place over time and continue to unfold, often focusing on the causes and effects of past events. The Internet offers many excellent sites that address various aspects of historical inquiry and encourage active learning.

History Wired

http://historywired.si.edu/about.cfm

This site allows visitors to take a virtual tour of the Smithsonian Institution's objects of interest. The interactive site map allows visitors to search by selecting dates on a time line, by selecting a broad category, or by a keyword search. Information is presented as though offered in a real life tour with a Smithsonian curator.

 II V VI

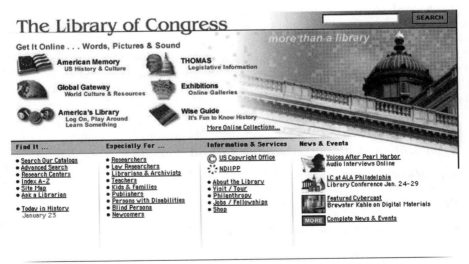

The Library of Congress

http://www.loc.gov

This site includes a number of exhibitions and American treasures from the collections of the Library of Congress. The American Memory section includes a large number of digitized historical collections in both audio and visual formats. When entering the Library of Congress page, the site map assists in navigating this resource.

 II VI

National Archives and Records Administration

http://www.archives.gov/index.html

Historical researchers will be able to explore *The Federal Register* online as well as famous speeches and images. The Online Exhibit Hall contains primary source documents such as the Magna Carta and the Constitution. Primary source lesson plans and activities for teachers and students can be found in the site's Digital Classroom.

 II X

The National Park Service

http://www.nps.gov

ParkNet provides links to the histories, cultures, and places of our nation's past. Facts on Civil War battlefields, landmarks, and museum collections are just some of the information you will find here. Questions about national parks, the National Park Service, or American history can be addressed online to National Park Service historians.

 II III

National Women's History Museum

http://www.nmwh.org

An in-depth history of the American women's suffrage movement is presented. The site contains a time line of major events in the women's rights movement from the World Anti-Slavery Convention of 1840 through the passage of the Nineteenth

Amendment. The online museum also contains an extensive image gallery and concluding interactive quiz about the site.

 II V VI X

The Valley of the Shadow: Two Communities in the American Civil War

http://jefferson.village.virginia.edu/vshadow2

This hypermedia archive examines one Northern and one Southern community using the backdrop of the Civil War. The site contains thousands of sources, such as religious documents, photographs, military records, and maps. In the Teaching Materials section, teachers can find lesson plans for social studies classes grades 7–12, and students can find paper topics for high school and college United States history courses.

 II III

Index of Resources for United States History

http://www.ukans.edu/history/VL/USA/

This site has connections to thousands of sites in United States history and other areas. The site is maintained by the University of Kansas Department of History and Lehrstuhl für Ältere deutsche Literaturwissenschaft der Universität Regensburg in German. The United States section is organized chronologically as well as by special topics. For example, visitors can explore links organized as the 1930s Great Depression and New Deal as well as links to Maritime History. The site also contains a large collection of databases, Internet indexes, and electronic texts.

 II

The Native American History Archive

http://www.ilt.columbia.edu/k12/naha/index.html

This site contains the Native American Navigator, which allows students to access a vast array of maps, documents, curricular materials, and a time line on topics related to Native American history and culture in the United States. The Native American History Archive Inquirer allows students to engage in constructivist and collaborative activities.

 II III V

The History Channel

http://www.historychannel.com

Students can feel a personal connection to history by exploring This Day In History, which provides information on Wall Street History, Automotive History, Civil War History, and General History. The link "What Happened on Your Birthday?" allows people to find historical events and individuals that are connected to their birthday. The site also maintains a number of interactive exhibits on topics such as Ellis Island and The Star Spangled Banner. Teachers from around the country who use The History Channel share ideas for lessons and projects.

 II

Smithsonian Institution National Museum of American History

http://www.americanhistory.si.edu/

An interactive time line allows exploration of the American heritage through objects found in the museum's collections and exhibits. The site houses a wide array of virtual exhibitions spanning all aspects of American history. These exhibitions have included Edison After Forty, Between a Rock and a Hard Place: A History of American Sweatshops, 1820–Present, and The 1896 Washington Salon & Art Photographic Exhibition. A highlight of the site is the interactive program You Be the Historian. This link allows study of secondary and primary sources and facilitates historical processing skills.

 II

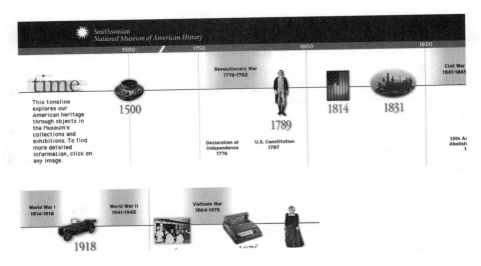

Smithsonian Institution National Museum of the American Indian

http://www.nmai.si.edu/

This site contains the NMAI Conexus which extends the walls of the museum through the World Wide Web. The NAMI Conexus shares the work of Native American artists with the public. Visitors can explore archives of past exhibits, various artists-in-residence, special events, and visiting artists.

I II V

The History Place

http://www.historyplace.com/

Highlights include an historical photo and speech of the week. Students can find homework tips on how to write a better history paper. There is a comprehensive gallery of presidential portraits as well as sounds of the presidents. A presentation on child labor in America 1908–1912 includes a number of primary source photographs.

II

Core Documents of United States Democracy

http://www.access.gpo.gov/su_docs/locators/coredocs/index.html

This site provides direct online access to current and historical government documents. These publications provide information about government activities and inform the electorate about the democratic process. This online forum allows free and immediate access to authenticated versions of these core documents of democracy.

 II VI X

Additional United States History and Cultures Web Sites

Archiving Early America

http://earlyamerica.com

50 States

http://www.50states.com

Discovery Channel American History Sites

http://www.discoveryschool.com/schrockguide/history/hista.html

Historical Text Archive

http://historicaltextarchive.com/

Historical Text Archive: United States History

http://historicaltextarchive.com/sections.php?op= listarticles&secid= 17

Historical Text Archive: Women's History

http://historicaltextarchive.com/links.php?op= viewlink&cid= 20

Historical Text Archive: African American History

http://historicaltextarchive.com/sections.php?op= listarticles&secid= 8

Black History
http://www.kn.pacbell.com/wired/BHM/AfroAm.html

National Latino Communication Center
http://www.nlcc.com

Lewis and Clark Expedition
http://www.pbs.org/lewisandclark/

The Library of Congress: Today in History.
http://lcweb2.loc.gov/ammem/today/today.html

Chinese-American History Timeline 1848 through 1995
http://online.sfsu.edu/~ericmar/catimeline.html

WestWeb
http://www.library.csi.cuny.edu/westweb/

Abraham Lincoln Online
http://www.netins.net/showcase/creative/lincoln.html

Caleb Johnson's Mayflower Web Pages
http://members.aol.com/calebj/mayflower.html

The Civil War Home Page
http://www.civil-war.net/

Colonial Williamsburg
http://www.history.org/

Hispanics in American Defense
http://www.neta.com/~1stbooks/defense.htm

Benjamin Franklin: A Documentary History
http://www.english.udel.edu/lemay/franklin/

1755—The French and Indian War
http://web.syr.edu/~laroux/

Hispanics in American History: Marshall Bernardo de Gálvez, Governor of the Spanish Louisiana

http://coloquio.com/famosos/galvezfa.html

The Oregon Trail

http://www.oregon-trail.com

United States Air Force Museum

http://www.wpafb.af.mil/museum/index.htm

University of North Carolina at Chapel Hill's Documenting the American South

http://metalab.unc.edu/docsouth/

The Virginia Center for Digital History

http://jefferson.village.virginia.edu/vcdh/

Teaching with Historic Places

http://www.cr.nps.gov/nr/twhp

Virtual Ellis Island Tour

http://www.capital.net/~alta/index.html

Crisis at Fort Sumter

http://www.tulane.edu/~latner/Union.In.Peril/Union_in_Peril.html

Great Chicago Fire and the Web of Memory

http://www.chicagohistory.org/fire/

History Channel Classroom

http://historychannel.com/classroom/index.html

NOVA Online Teachers Site

http://www.pbs.org/wgbh/nova/teachers/

Virtual Jamestown

http://jefferson.village.virginia.edu/vcdh/jamestown/

Virtual Marching Tour of the American Revolution

http://www.ushistory.org/march/index.html

National Women's History Museum
http://www.nmwh.org/

Documents for the Study of American History
http://www.ukans.edu/carrie/docs/amdocs_index.html

Center for History and New Media
http://chnm.gmu.edu/index1.html

CHAPTER 4

World History and Cultures

GENERAL HISTORY SITES

The World Wide Web (WWW) offers teachers of world history and cultures a dizzying array of sites that feature informational articles, accessible images, and virtual field trips to other countries and other time periods. General world history and cultures sites are listed first, followed by sites on specific regions of the world.

Mr. Donn's World History Resources

http://members.aol.com/MrDonnHistory/World.html

This excellent gateway site covers traditional topics such as the history of specific periods, events, and people. Contemporary topics such as terrorism and women's history are also included. Truly novel are options for time lines, world holidays, and free worksheets as well as links to online services and other resources about history.

 I II IX

Histor eSearch.com

http://www.snowcrest.net/jmike

Intended for both students and educators, this is a comprehensive site featuring hundreds of links to sites related to modern and ancient world history, medieval history, Latin American history, and African history, among others.

 I II IX X

BBC Modern World History

http://www.bbc.co.uk/education/modern/

This site maintained by the British Broadcasting Corporation features interactive animations, including animated maps and time lines (animation requires

Shockwave software, which is available on the site). The teacher's section provides lessons, further resources, and links to related sites.

 I II IX

The History Channel

http://www.historychannel.com

In addition to articles, historic speeches, and video clips, this site offers hundreds of links to other history-related sites. Students will enjoy the What Happened on Your Birthday? feature, and teachers will find study guides, quizzes, and teaching ideas in "Classroom."

 I II IX

| Articles, E-Mail and Web Links About History

Articles, E-Mail and Web Links About History

Reprinted with permission of Middleweb.com.

MiddleWeb History and Social Studies Resources

http://www.middleweb.com/CurrSocStud.html

This gateway site provides access to a number of world history links. Topics include the origins of humankind, a virtual autopsy of a preserved Incan, ancient and medieval history, and teaching about the Holocaust.

 I II IX

Kathy Schrock's Guide for Educators: World and Ancient History

http://discoveryschool.com/schrockguide/history/histw.html

This excellent site should be the first place world history teachers visit. In addition to covering virtually all related topics extensively, it offers useful features and information, such as lesson plans, web links, discussions, and images.

 I II IX

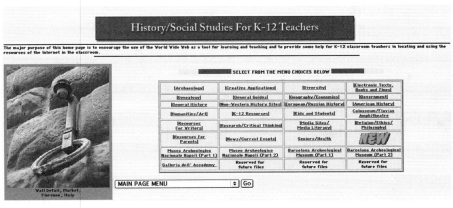

Reprinted with permission of Dennis A. Boals.

History/Social Studies Web Site for K–12 Teachers

http://www.execpc.com/~dboals/boals.html

Provides assistance to K–12 teachers in locating WWW resources for the teaching of history. Topics include archaeology, European history, non-Western history, and the humanities and art. The Non-Western History Sites section features comprehensive links for the study of Asia, Africa, Central and South America, the Middle East, India, and others.

 I II IX

Awesome Library: K–12 Social Studies Lesson Plans

http://www.awesomelibrary.org/social.html

Topics include general history resources, multicultural activities, and multidisciplinary lessons. Particularly useful is the breakdown for elementary teachers, for teens, and for secondary teachers.

 I II IX

EDSITEment

http://edsitement.neh.fed.us

Sponsored in part by the National Endowment for the Humanities, this site includes lesson plans, learning guides, and links to the top humanities sites on the web. Of particular interest are the links to top museums, libraries, and cultural institutions.

 I II IX

Tales of Wonder

http://www.darsie.net/talesofwonder

This award-winning collection of folk and fairy tales has representative stories from virtually all countries of the world and underscores humanity's common heritage of storytelling.

 I II IX

World History Archives

http://www.hartford-hwp.com/archives

This gateway site offers documents and images from ancient to contemporary times. In addition to broad topics such as politics and war, the economy, and the environment, users can access documents by world region.

 I II IX

Historical Documents on the Internet

http://www.cssjournal.com/hisdoc.html

This collection of resources to aid in the study and teaching of world history includes images, online documents, and links to library collections, university web pages, and Internet resources. It is maintained by *The Computers in the Social Studies* electronic journal.

I II IX

Internet Modern History Sourcebook

http://www.fordham.edu/halsall/mod/modsbook.html

Thousands of resources, links, and multimedia (video clips, pictures, and audio) on a variety of historical topics and epochs. Also available are sourcebooks on ancient, African, Islamic, Jewish, and women's history.

 I II IX

Ancient World Web

http://www.julen.net/aw

Provides the kind of information students often ask about: daily life, mythology and religion, archaeology, and art, to name a few. Location of resources is greatly facilitated by a meta index, a geography index, and a subject index.

   I II IX

Exploring Ancient World Cultures

http://eawc.evansville.edu

This introduction to ancient world cultures on the WWW begins with an excellent essay entitled "Why Study Ancient World Cultures?" useful in developing a rationale for students. Topics include the Near East, India, Egypt, China, Greece, Rome, Islam, and Europe.

   I II IX

Ancient World History: Omaha Public Library

http://www.omaha.lib.ne.us/subjects/society/history/ancienthis.shtml

Teachers of young students will find helpful information, lesson plans, and links in this site. In particular, connections to literature, virtual activities, and information about daily life topics (such as toys, pets, clothing, and hairstyles) are useful tools.

     I II IX

HyperHistory Online

http://www.hyperhistory.com

A collection of time lines that graphically display 3,000 years of world history. The organization allows viewers to compare the relationships among people, places, and events throughout history. Interlinked maps provide geographic context. Users can also link to over 300 related web sites.

 I II IX

A Teacher's Guide to the Holocaust

http://fcit.coedu.usf.edu/holocaust

Classroom activities, web links, music, photographs, and art are just some of the resources available on this impressive site.

 I II IX

Art History Resources on the Web

http://witcombe.bcpw.sbc.edu/ARTHLinks.html

The study of history can be greatly enhanced by the inclusion of art. This site has links to galleries and resources, and users can even access images of art produced in prehistoric times through the twentieth century.

 I II IX

AFRICA AND THE MIDDLE EAST

Reprinted with permission of the Center for Middle Eastern Studies.

Middle East Network Information Center

http://menic.utexas.edu/mes.html

In addition to a country index, users can access contents by subject (such as ancient history, arts and humanities, religion, and energy). Teachers will find useful the K–12 educational resources and electronic publishing features.

    I II III IX

K–12 Electronic Guide for African Resources on the Internet

http://www.sas.upenn.edu/African_Studies/Home_Page/AFR_GIDE.html

Annotated listing of resource-full sites for use in the study and teaching of Africa. In addition to country-by-country information, there is data about the history, languages, and environment of Africa. Especially useful for educators is the Multimedia Archives section, which features maps and satellite images, flags, and photographs.

 I II III IX

H-Afrteach

http://www.h-net.msu.edu/~afrteach

This discussion list caters to educators and students interested in African studies. In addition to lesson plans, course syllabi, and other instructional materials, users can access images, folk tales, and timely book reviews.

 I II IX

Africa-Related Links

http://polyglot.lss.wisc.edu/afrst/links.html

The University of Wisconsin–Madison's African Studies Program provides hundreds of links to resources on the WWW. Topics include news, politics, art, languages, literature, and more. Of special interest to educators is the K–12 Resources and Instructional Materials section.

 I II IX

Non-Western History: Africa

http://www.execpc.com/~dboals/africa.html#AFRICA

Part of the History/Social Studies Web Site for K–12 Teachers, the Africa section is rich with links to museums, exhibits, news services, and art and music resources.

 I II IX

Non-Western History: Middle East

http://www.execpc.com/~dboals/m-east.html#MIDDLE EAST

Part of the History/Social Studies Web Site for K–12 Teachers, the Middle East section offers personal diaries, ancient texts, clip art, and historical documents.

 I II IX

Little Horus

http://www.horus.ics.org.eg/

Especially appropriate for elementary school students, users take a tour of Egypt, where they learn about its history, geography, and entertainment. The bilingual site (English and Arabic) boasts over 3,000 pages of information and graphics.

 I II III IX

USAID Bureau for Africa

http://www.info.usaid.gov/regions/afr

Contains information on development activities in Africa. For educators and students, the most helpful features present country-by-country data, the status of education, and environmental concerns.

 I II III IX

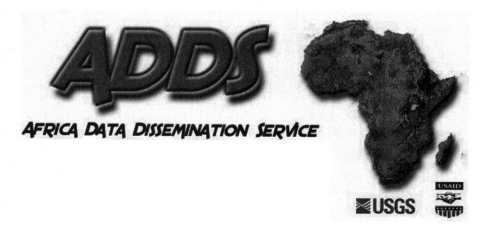

African Studies Internet Resources

http://www.columbia.edu/cu/lweb/indiv/Africa/cuvl

A wealth of resources and links for both students and teachers. Resources are broken down by region and country, organizations, and topics. Teaching resources include K–12 curriculum materials.

 I II III IX

Africa Data Dissemination Service

http://edcintl.cr.usgs.gov/adds

For each African region and its countries, a wealth of information is provided. Images from satellites, country statistics, national and local maps, flags, history, and development efforts are included.

 I II III IX

ASIA AND THE PACIFIC

Ask Asia

http://www.askasia.org

Multimedia site on a wide range of topics related to the history, culture, and politics of Asia. Includes lessons, images, photos, and maps that can be downloaded and used in K–12 classrooms. Also provides a link to Asia Source, a searchable database on current events in the region.

 I II III IX

Asian Studies WWW Virtual Library

http://coombs.anu.edu.au/WWWVL-AsianStudies.html

Exhaustive annotated listings and links to resources on the region as a whole and on individual countries and topics. Users can also access information by the individual country and territory listings.

 I II IX

Non-Western History: Asia/Pacific, China/Japan, and India

http://www.execpc.com/~dboals/hist.html

Part of the History/Social Studies Web Site for K–12 Teachers. Users can select specific parts of the world to explore. Links to history sites, maps, clip art, memoirs, and historical documents are just a few of the resources included.

 I II IX

India & China in Comparative and Global Perspective

http://www.csupomona.edu/~inch/

Showcases curriculum projects created by teachers involved in a three-year professional development program on India and China. Links to selected Internet sites about Asia are also provided.

 I II IX

China on the Net

http://www.kn.pacbell.com/wired/China/hotlist.html

Comprehensive list of Internet links for the study of China. Students will appreciate learning pages such as Treasure Hunt, Multimedia Scrapbook, and Web Quest. Features include virtual tours, Chinese culture and proverbs, religions, human rights, the environment, and the visual arts. "Searching for China" is a role-playing/simulation activity that teaches students about the complexities of the country.

 I II III IX

Pacific Internet Sites

http://www.nla.gov.au/oz/pacsites.html

Links to reference material, news sources, electronic journals, and more—all related to the Pacific.

 I II IX

Pacific Islands Internet Resources

http://www2.hawaii.edu/~ogden/piir/index.html

Links to WWW resources focusing on the Pacific Islands, including media resources, document collections, maps, and images.

 I II IX

EUROPE

Multnomah County Library

http://www.multcolib.org/homework/eurohist.html

Extensive collection of links to European history topics and images. The 3,500 K–12 resources were reviewed and selected by educators and librarians. Topics include medieval history, rulers, speeches, and biographies.

    I II IX

The Holocaust World Resource Center

http://www.hwrc.org

This nonprofit educational site is an international center for Holocaust resources. Different areas related to Eastern European Jewry are included.

  I II IX

Academic Info: European History

http://www.academicinfo.net/histeuro.html

This site offers links to specific topics such as Spanish history, WWI, and the Cold War, as well as portals to megasites on European history.

I II III IX

Europe/Russia/Eastern Europe

http://www.execpc.com/~dboals/europe.html

Part of the larger site, History/Social Studies Web Site for K–12 Teachers. Users can access information pertaining to topics such as ancient and classical history, medieval times, the Renaissance and Reformation, and the modern world.

 I II IX

WWW Virtual Library: West European Studies

http://www.library.pitt.edu/subject_guides/westeuropean/wwwes/

Comprehensive guide to Internet resources on Western Europe. The search engine allows searches by academic discipline. Also included are regional current events.

 I II IX

Yale University Library: European History & West European Studies

http://www.library.yale.edu/Internet/eurohist.html

A variety of links to electronic resources concerning the history of Europe.

 I II IX

Women in Modern European History

http://www.barbwired.com/nadiaweb/mehap/links.html

Alphabetical links to women in history as well as information on the suffragist movement and women in the world history curriculum.

 I II IX

Revelations

from the

Russian Archives

Revelations from the Russian Archives

http://lcweb.loc.gov/exhibits/archives/intro.html

Unique Library of Congress site focusing on twentieth-century Russia. Lots of information on the internal workings of the Soviet system and its relations with the United States.

 I II IX

USAID Regions: Europe & Eurasia

http://www.usaid.gov/regions/europe_eurasia

Links to information on all the countries in Europe and the former Soviet Union.

 I II IX

The Holocaust: A Learning Site for Students

http/www.ushmm.org/outreach

The U.S. Holocaust Memorial Museum's site provides students and teachers with text, maps, historical photographs and images of artifacts, and audio clips. The detailed visual time line facilitates student understanding of how events unfolded.

 I II IX

LATIN AMERICA AND THE CARIBBEAN

ENGLISH | ESPAÑOL

[HLAS Online Home Page | Search HLAS Online | Help | FAQ | Comments]

Handbook of Latin American Studies

http://lcweb2.loc.gov/hlas

Annotated bibliography on Latin America. Updated monthly, it provides access to all volumes since its first publication in 1935.

 I II IX

WWW Virtual Library: Latin American Studies

http://lanic.utexas.edu/las.html

Excellent database of resources and links about Latin American studies. Users can select specific countries or access information by subject. The K–12 feature is particularly helpful for educators.

 I II IX

Non-Western History: Central/South America

http://www.execpc.com/~dboals/s-amer.html#1CENTRAL/SOUTH

Exhaustive annotated listing of links to Internet resources. Selections include biographies, visual arts, maps, and famous speeches.

 I II IX

Latin World

http://www.latinworld.com

A directory of Internet resources on Latin America and the Caribbean. Although a large part of this bilingual site focuses on trade and commerce, information on cultural traditions, history, and government is also provided. The search engine facilitates access of data and images. Latin World Kids provides links to educational, arts and literature, and Ask the Expert sites.

 I II IX

USAID Regions: Latin America and the Caribbean

http://www.info.usaid.gov/regions/lac

Information on selected countries in Latin America and the Caribbean. Most useful is the current data on social and economic indicators.

 I II III IX

SICE: Foreign Trade Information Service

http://www.sice.oas.org

Maintained by the Organization of American States, this trilingual site offers the latest information on international trade issues. The site map provides detailed, country-specific data on all its members.

 I II IX

Association Of Caribbean States	Asociación de Estados del Caribe	Association des Etats de La Caraïbe
English	Español	Français

Americas Society

http://www.americas-society.org

Resources and information about the Western Hemisphere (including Canada, Latin America, and the Caribbean), especially in the arts, literature, and music.

 I II IX

Additional World History and Cultures Web Sites

Africa Quest

http://africaquest.classroom.com

AfroCuba Web

http://afrocubaweb.com

Atlas of the Greek and Roman World

http://www.unc.edu/depts/cl_atlas

Art and Life in Africa Project

http://www.uiowa.edu/~africart

Collapse: Why Do Civilizations Fall?

http://www.learner.org/exhibits/collapse

Encyclopedia Mythica

http://www.pantheon.org

History On-Line

http://www.historian.org

The Great War

http://www.pbs.org/greatwar

Internext Gateway to South Africa

http://minotaur.marques.co.za

K–12 History on the Internet Resource Guide
http://www.xs4all.nl/~swanson/history

Perseus Digital Project
http://www.perseus.tufts.edu

Polynesian Cultural Center
http://www.polynesia.com

Religious History
http://www.georgetown.edu/labyrinth/subjects/relig/relig.html

Renaissance: What Inspired This Age of Balance and Order?
http://www.learner.org/exhibits/renaissance

Social Studies School Service: Ancient History
http://socialstudies.com/c/@0/Pages/ancienthistory.html

Springfield Township High School Virtual Library: World History
http://mciunix.mciu.k12.pa.us/~spjvweb/stuworld.html

WWW-VL History: Central Catalogue
http://www.ukans.edu/history/VL

CHAPTER 5

Government and Law

The best way to study how government works is by watching the government itself in action. The World Wide Web (WWW) now gives direct access to national, state, and local government agencies, where students and teachers can both observe and participate in government activities online.

National Archives and Records Administration (NARA)

http://www.archives.gov/index.html

The National Archives, the official repository of U.S. government documents, provides a treasure trove of material for teaching government and history. The Online Exhibit Hall shows hundreds of original documents as diverse as the Declaration of Independence, the Constitution of the United States of America, World War II posters, and "When Nixon Met Elvis." The Research Room provides excellent guidance on searching and obtaining records from NARA's vast library of documents, and the Digital Classroom provides primary source documents and instructional activities employing materials from the National Archives. High-interest documents (such as the Apollo 11 flight plan) are featured monthly, along with instructional materials and research tips. From NARA's web site, each of the U.S. presidential libraries is just one click away.

 II IV VI X

Thomas

http://thomas.loc.gov

Thomas, a huge and successful undertaking of the Library of Congress, provides full access to legislative information on the Internet. This vast site includes the text of bills before Congress, voting records of legislators, records of committee activity, the full text of the *Congressional Record,* and hundreds of other resources for students of government and their teachers. This is a one-stop resource for information about the functioning of the legislative branch of the U.S. government.

 II V VI X

Your Guide to the U.S. Government

http://www.whitehouse/government/

A service of the White House, this site allows users to search and subscribe to White House publications, search the White House web site, search all government web sites, or even look for a job in government. Most of the services provided are actually links to other government web sites, but this is a convenient and easy-to-use place to begin.

 II V VI X

FirstGov

http://www.firstgov.gov/

This portal site is a gateway to all government agencies and services for citizens and businesses. It includes federal, state, local, and tribal agencies and provides access to everything from passport applications and social security information to lottery results.

 VI X

Keeping America Informed

http://www.access.gpo.gov

Virtually every piece of paper the government produces is printed by the U.S. Government Printing Office. Most of the recent materials are available online with full instructions for downloading them on a personal computer. Others are available at very low cost. Topics include the judge's opinion in *United States v. Microsoft,* economic indicators, and the entire federal budget. Search and browse features make this an easy site to use.

 VI X

Ben's Guide to the U. S. Government for Kids

http://bensguide.gpo.gov/

This engaging portal site provides kids with access to the government agencies that will be useful to them for school or community projects. It covers such topics as Our Nation, Historical Documents, Branches of Government, How Laws are Made, and many more in an attractive, kid-friendly format.

     VI X

Fed World Information Network

www.fedworld.gov

A project of the U.S. Department of Commerce, Fed World is an information network that links you to thousands of federal resources on the Internet. This is a great place for students to check out the federal jobs that are available anywhere in the nation.

 V VI X

Archiving Early America

http://earlyamerica.com

   This site provides high-quality digital primary source material from eighteenth-century America. Original newspapers, maps, and writings are shown on the computer screen much as they appeared more than 200 years ago. This is a must-visit site for teachers interested in document analysis approaches to social studies.

 II VI X

Avalon Project at the Yale Law School: Documents in Law, History, and Diplomacy

http://www.yale.edu/lawweb/avalon/avalon.htm

   This award-winning site provides full-text documents that are foundational to the study of American democracy, from the Code of Hammurabi (B.C. 1750) to the executive order establishing the Office of Homeland Security (2001). This site is truly astonishing for its depth and ease of use.

 I V VI X

Additional Government Web Sites

Infoplease from Lycos on U.S. Government and History

http://infoplease.lycos.com/ipa/A0101021.html

Ask ERIC Lesson Plans: Civics and Government

http://askeric.org/cgi-bin/lessons.cgi/Social_Studies

EXECUTIVE BRANCH

The executive branch of the federal government consists of the offices of the president and vice president, cabinet officers, and all of their respective departments, bureaus, and agencies.

The White House

http://www.whitehouse.gov

Not only is the White House the home of the president of the United States, but it is also the seat of the executive branch of the government. This site gives rich information about the offices of the president and vice president, the history of these offices, and the story of the White House itself as a historical building. There is also a feature page on the First Lady and a section on the family living quarters.

 II V VI X

White House for Kids

http://www.whitehouse.gov/kids/

A special section of the White House web site is devoted to kids. From this site, kids can make the acquaintance of pets in the White House, contact the President or Vice President, take a quiz from India, the cat, or read stories about kids in history. This is a charming and engaging site for elementary students in particular.

 II V VI X

U.S. Department of State

http://www.state.gov

The Department of State's web site offers a rich array of resources on America's foreign policy and relations with foreign governments. One of the most visited sections is Travel Warnings and Consular Information Sheets. Warnings sheets provide snapshots of some of the world's most troubled nations and regions, and Consular Information sheets give details on immigration practices, health issues, political disturbances, currency regulations, crime and security, drug information, and the stability of government services for every nation in the world. A new feature is a web site devoted to Cuba and our relations with that island neighbor. A special section of the web site provides resources for teachers and their students on the history of diplomacy, career information in diplomacy, and links to diplomatic and geographic information sites across the Internet.

 I III V VI VII IX X

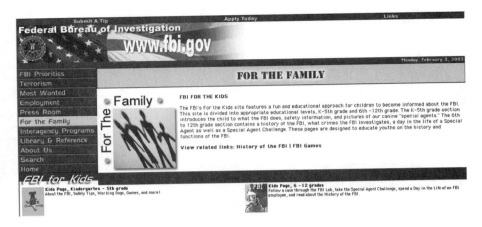

Federal Bureau of Investigation (FBI)

http://www.fbi.gov

The FBI page offers valuable information about crime investigation in the United States and how the federal agency assists local police in solving crimes. The famous "Ten Most Wanted" list is available on this site, as are stories of major ongoing investigations. The FBI for Kids page features information on crime detection and crime prevention as well as games and activities related to law enforcement. Age-appropriate games, lessons, and features cover topics such as fingerprints, crime-fighting dogs, and the chemistry of crime. Special links to other educational web sites are also provided for teachers and parents.

 V VI VII X

U.S. Department of Justice

http://www.usdoj.gov/kidspage

The Department of Justice's Justice for Kids & Youth web site is an informative resource on the courts and the law, crime prevention, and civil rights. In addition to providing special features for children, this site links teachers and parents to instructional resources on topics such as tolerance, health and safety, and current events, as well as topics linked specifically to social studies: criminology, human relations, government, technology, and history.

 V VI VIII X

Central Intelligence Agency (CIA)

http://www.cia.gov/cia/ciakids/index.html

The CIA's *World Fact Book* is a veritable textbook for area studies, geopolitics, and contemporary world history. Entries for every nation contain current maps and information on the geography, people, government, economy, communications, transportation, and military, as well as transnational issues. In a world where borders and alliances change daily, the *World Fact Book* alone would be worth a visit, but there is even more. Games include "Try a Disguise," "Code Warriors," and word puzzles. There is a colorful history of espionage, intelligence, and the agency and a special feature on the CIA's Canine Corps. A link back to the CIA main page leads to more sophisticated information for older students, including instructions for obtaining declassified intelligence documents.

      I III V VI VIII IX X

U.S. Census Bureau

http://www.census.gov

The Census Bureau web site provides access to the most comprehensive statistical information imaginable about the United States and its people. Users can search for and arrange data in ways that answer specific questions about conditions and trends in the United States. Especially helpful for teachers is the site's Gazetteer, with map-drawing capability for any site in the United States included in the Census, from Los Angeles, California, to Ten Sleep, Wyoming. Go to For Teachers for teaching materials and publications suitable for use in K–12 classrooms.

    I III V VI X

Additional Executive Branch Web Sites

U.S. Department of Agriculture

http://www.usda.gov

U.S. Department of Commerce

http://www.doc.gov

U.S. Department of Defense

http://www.defenselink.mil

U.S. Department of Education

http://www.ed.gov

U.S. Department of Energy

http://www.energy.gov

U.S. Department of Health and Human Services

http://www.dhhs.gov

U.S. Department of Housing and Urban Development

http://www.hud.gov

U.S. Department of the Interior

http://www.doi.gov

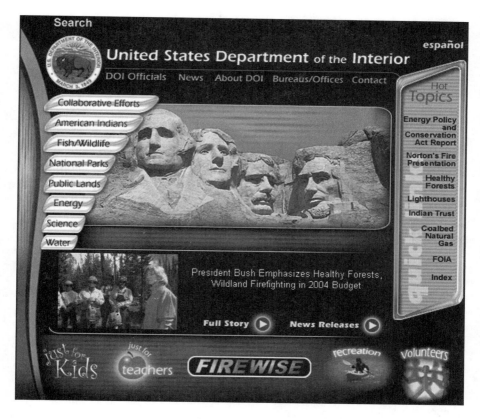

U.S. Department of Labor
http://www.dol.gov

U.S. Department of Transportation
http://www.dot.gov

U.S. Department of Veterans Affairs
http://www.va.gov

U.S. Office of Management and Budget
http://www.whitehouse.gov/OMB

LEGISLATIVE BRANCH

The legislative branch of the federal government consists of the House of Representatives and the Senate. Both bodies provide excellent resources for the study of government and the legislative process.

U.S. House of Representatives

http://www.house.gov

The House site gives access to congressional representatives as well as information about current deliberations and votes. Linked to the home page is an excellent document on "The Legislative Process" and the protocols and operations of the House.

 V VI X

The U.S. House Of Representatives Educational Resources

This area provides access to documents related to the legislative process that are of interest to the public.

Available Educational Resources

Tying It All Together
    The legislative process is explained.
How Our Laws Are Made
    A detailed description of the legislative process.

U.S. House of Representatives: Educational Resources

http://www.house.gov/house/Educat.html

A special section of the House of Representatives web site provides educational resources on the legislative process, how laws are made, the Declaration of Independence, and the Constitution, as well as historical information about the House and its role in the Republic.

 II V VI X

U.S. Senate

http://www.senate.gov

Contact a senator, track a presidential nomination, follow activity on the Senate floor, or check on committee actions on this attractive and well-designed web site. Students and teachers can also find interesting and engaging materials on the history of the Senate, its art collection, and myths and falsehoods about the Senate and its members, past and present. Click on Learning About the Senate to explore the Senate's legislative process, check out frequently asked questions, or e-mail a question to the Senate historian or curator.

 II V VI X

JUDICIAL BRANCH

The judicial branch of government is made up of the Supreme Court and all other courts in the federal system. Because federal, state, and local court systems are linked by the appeals process, the resources in this section are selected to provide social studies teachers with information about all levels of the legal system in the United States.

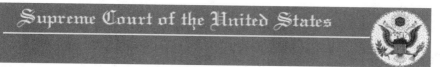

U.S. Supreme Court

http://www.supremecourtus.gov/

The Supreme Court home page links the viewer to information which provides an overview of the Supreme Court, the docket, the court schedule, opinions, and other helpful resources.

 V VI X

Oyez Project: Northwestern University

http://oyez.nwu.edu

The Oyez Project is one of the most comprehensive resources imaginable on the Supreme Court of the United States. It provides full-text versions of written arguments, decisions, and dissenting opinions. Most intriguing are the recordings of actual oral arguments, which can be heard through computer sound systems using Real Audio®. This is a vast, attractive, and interactive site that allows teachers to explore very serious and important content in a manageable way.

 V VI X

Legal Information Institute

Legal Information Institute: Cornell University Law School

http://www.law.cornell.edu

This comprehensive search site provides access to a large array of resources for legal scholars, students, and teachers. Its sophisticated search capacity links users to laws about virtually any topic affecting contemporary life and provides excellent coverage of U.S. Supreme Court decisions as well as state and local court opinions. One of its most interesting features for social studies teachers is access to constitutional and legal information from nations around the globe.

 V VI IX X

Findlaw

http:/www.findlaw.com

FindLaw is focused on law and government and provides access to a comprehensive, growing library of legal resources useful to legal professionals, teachers, consumers, and small businesses. FindLaw's mission is to make legal information on the Internet easy to find. For teachers and students, this site provides access to legal information on hundreds of topics as well as information about legal careers and legal help for families and community members.

 V VI X

National Law-Related Education Resource Center

http://www.abanet.org/publiced/nlrc.html

The National Law-Related Education Resource Center provides an excellent gateway to dozens of Internet resources for law-related education for children and youth. From this site, teachers can order the *LRE Report,* the nation's leading newsletter on issues, trends, and people in law-related education.

 V VI X

Court TV Online

http://www.courttv.com

Sometimes controversial, often provocative, but always an engaging and intriguing look at contemporary legal issues, trials, and crime. This commercial site provides background information and up-to-the-minute reporting on current legal proceedings (mostly criminal cases), along with interviews of key players in high-profile cases, blunt commentary, and debates by legal experts in specialized fields. This site is most suitable for adults and older students.

 V VI X

Office of Juvenile Justice and Delinquency Prevention (OJJDP), U.S. Department of Justice

http://ojjdp.ncjrs.org

The OJJDP web site is designed to provide information and resources on juvenile crime and communities' work to create safe environments for children and youth. This site includes a full-text version of the 1999 report on juvenile crime and victimization.

 V VI X

American Civil Liberties Union (ACLU)

http://www.aclu.org

The Constitution authorizes the government to act, and the Bill of Rights limits that ability in very specific ways. The ACLU is a public interest organization devoted exclusively to protecting the basic civil liberties guaranteed in the Bill of Rights. In its almost seven decades in existence, the ACLU has become a national institution; its web site reflects its long history and its complex, and often controversial, agenda. From a strictly rights-oriented point of view, the ACLU site offers resources and commentary on dozens of the most difficult legal issues facing this nation, including abortion, gay rights, the death penalty, racial equality, students' rights, and privacy. It is direct, forthright, and uncompromising. Older students love it.

 V VI X

Street Law

www.streetlaw.org

An outgrowth of Georgetown University's practical law program, first taught in Washington, D.C., schools over 20 years ago, Street Law is a "nonprofit organization dedicated to empowering people through law-related education." It offers instructional materials and student texts as well as information about the legal system to educators at all levels of the system.

 V VI X

National Crime Prevention Council

http://www.ncpc.org

The group that brought us McGruff, the crime-fighting dog, sponsors this lively web site, which contains very helpful information about crime awareness and community involvement in crime prevention. A new focus on school safety and safe behavior in the community is particularly helpful for younger children, and the council's crime watch programs are often used as public service projects for older students.

 V VI X

Additional Law and Court Web Site

Emory Law Library Federal Courts Finder

http://www.law.emory.edu/FEDCTS

LOCAL GOVERNMENT

Most experience with government is at the local level. These sites put teachers and students in touch with both state and local governments.

States News Service

http://www.statesnews.org

Produced and updated weekly by the Council of State Governments, this very informative site covers government activity in all of the states, possessions, and territories. Especially interesting is its coverage of the effects of federal legislation and mandates on state and local governments. From this helpful site, students and teachers can follow links to web sites for all 50 states, Guam, and Puerto Rico.

 V VI X

State and Local Governments

http://lcweb.loc.gov/global/state

A service of the Library of Congress, this site offers a comprehensive catalog of links to state and local government resources, including state maps and links to the web sites of state and local government agencies.

 V VI X

INTERNATIONAL AFFAIRS AND ORGANIZATIONS

National governments attempt to secure their mutual defense, promote peace, and assist in the development of all nations through international organizations. For the United States, two of the most important of these agencies are the North Atlantic Treaty Organization (NATO) and the United Nations (UN).

United Nations

Peace and Security

Economic and Social Development

International Law

Human Rights

Humanitarian Affairs

United Nations

http:/www.un.org

The web site provides access to information about the UN's history and achievements as well as its ongoing programs in peace and security, international law, humanitarian affairs, human rights, and economic and social development. Online full-text documents allow students to track UN peacekeeping and relief missions, and high-quality maps are provided for each of the member countries and the UN mission sites.

 II III V VI IX

UNICEF—Voices of Youth

http://www.unicef.org/voy

The United Nations International Children's Emergency Fund (UNICEF) provides Voices of Youth, an informative and engaging opportunity to help students develop awareness of issues and crises confronting children and youth throughout the world. The Meeting Place gives students a chance to interact with other young people around the world through a bulletin board system that often carries powerful and wrenching messages from children in warring or disaster-torn countries. The Learning Place is an online resource students can use to learn about world issues and crises, and The Teachers' Place provides instructional materials and guidance for teachers who wish to explore the rights of children in their classes.

 I III V VI IX

Foreign Affairs Guide to International Affairs on the Internet

http://www.foreignaffairs.org/WAClinks.html

This venerable journal's web site serves as an easy-to-navigate portal to one of the most comprehensive listings of international affairs links on the Internet. It includes news services and international new agencies, think tanks and advocacy groups, and international organizations. This is an excellent first stop for teacher and student research on foreign affairs.

 I II V VI IX

WWW Virtual Library: International Affairs Resource—Elizabethtown College

http://www.etown.edu/vl

This superb web site provides access to new resources, including live international radio and television broadcasts, organizations such as the European Union and the United Nations, regional and national information, and information on global issues such as the environment, development, and human rights. This is a genuine foundational resource for the study of international affairs in social studies.

 I III V VI IX

InfoNation from the United Nations

http://www.un.org/Pubs/CyberSchoolBus/infonation/info.asp

InfoNation is an easy-to-use, two-step database that allows students and teachers to view and compare the most up-to-date statistical data for the member states of the United Nations. This is an excellent resource for student research or for inquiry lessons.

 I III V VI IX

Additional International Affairs and Organizations Web Sites

North Atlantic Treaty Organization (NATO)

http://www.nato.int

Electronic Embassy: A Resource of and for the Washington, D.C., Foreign Embassy Community

http://www.embassy.org

Embassy World: A Directory of All the World's Embassies and Consulates

http://www.embassyworld.com

Foreign Government Resources on the Web

http://www.lib.umich.edu/govdocs/foreign.html

Governments on the World Wide Web

http://www.gksoft.com/govt/en

Library of Congress Country Studies

http://lcweb2.loc.gov/frd/cs/cshome.html

Centre for Study of Diplomacy

http://www.le.ac.uk/dsp/mfas.html

Universal Currency Converter

http:/www.xe.net/ucc/full.shtml

Virtual Sources of Maps and Data

http://www.virtualsources.com

CHAPTER 6

Citizenship Education and Political Science

Full participation in a democratic society calls for informed participation in government, thoughtful voting, and insightful monitoring of government activity. The resources in this chapter help teachers foster those skills and attitudes among their students.

CIVIC IDEALS AND PRACTICES

Being a good citizen means participating knowledgeably in community and government affairs at all levels. These sites help teachers foster civic participation by individual students and entire classes.

Center for Civic Education

http://www.civiced.org

The Center for Civic Education is a nonprofit, nonpartisan educational corporation dedicated to fostering informed, responsible participation in civic life by citizens committed to democratic values and principles. Its easy-to-navigate site provides curricular materials, Internet links and resources, and articles and papers on civic education and responsible citizenship.

    V VI X

CivNet

http://www.civnet.org

At the heart of this site, sponsored by CIVITAS, an international organization devoted to civic education, is a monthly journal of articles about the state of democracy and civic education. Its civic education resource library features online links to lessons plans, syllabi, historical documents, journals, newsletters, and other materials. Civics teachers should bookmark this site.

   V VI X

Learning Adventures in Citizenship

http://www.thirteen.org/newyork/laic/index.html

Focused on New York and based on a documentary of that city's history, this site provides dozens of helpful suggestions for ways to incorporate local history into all programs and engage students in community affairs. The site features dozens of useful links to community resources all over the nation and offers lessons and teaching resources for social studies teachers at all levels.

   V VI IX X

Activism 2000 Project

http://www.youthactivism.com

Activism 2000 seeks to engage young people under the age of 18, "the 26% solution," in solving problems in their communities and our nation. Billed as a "Democracy Dropout Prevention Clearinghouse," this site provides help and information to parents, mentors, teachers, principals, policymakers, and other adult allies who want to collaborate with youth to achieve positive community change.

   V VI X

Internet Resources for Civic Educators

http://www.ed.gov/databases/ERIC_Digests/ed415176.html

The U.S. Department of Education provides a substantial listing of web sites and Internet resources that support civic education and citizen participation in community improvement. This digest describes a number of these helpful sites in detail.

     V VI X

American Promise

http://www.farmers.com/FarmComm/AmericanPromise/

Based on the popular KQED and PBS series, American Promise is a program from Farmers' Insurance that brings government to life by engaging students in the politicial process in their own classrooms. Themes include: Touchstones of Our Society, The Challenges We Face, Acting On These Ideas, and Keeping the Promise.

   V VI X

Additional Civic Ideals and Practices Web Sites

Closeup Foundation Online

http://www.closeup.org

Presidential Classroom Homepage

http://www.presidentialclassroom.org

POLITICAL SCIENCE

The central obligation of responsible citizenship is informed voting in local, state, and national elections. These sites focus on the political process and provide help for educators in teaching students about this critical form of participation in a democratic society.

Project Vote Smart

http://www.vote-smart.org

Vote Smart tracks the performance of over 13,000 government officials at the national, state, and local levels. It also provides engaging educational activities and teacher lessons that focus on how citizens can improve their representation in government affairs.

   V VI X

League of Women Voters

http://www.lwv.org

The League of Women Voters encourages informed, active participation by citizens in government, promotes understanding of public policy issues, and influences policy through public education and advocacy. The league provides its own materials on how to get involved as well as links to many other voter education sites.

     V VI X

Social Studies Sources

http://education.indiana.edu/~socialst

Hosted by Indiana University, this resource guide is part of a much more comprehensive gateway for social studies educators and students. It provides links to major political organizations as well as nonpartisan groups and political science scholars throughout the nation.

    V VI X

Rock the Vote

http://www.rockthevote.org

Founded by members of the recording industry to fight censorship, Rock the Vote is "dedicated to protecting freedom of expression and to helping young people realize and utilize their power to effect change in the civic and political lives of their communities." Much of this organization's focus is upon changing voter registration procedures to encourage greater participation by young people. It also provides guidance on how to influence the political process in local communities.

  V VI X

Teaching Politics: Techniques and Technologies

http://teachpol.tcnj.edu

Produced by Professor William Ball at the College of New Jersey, this site is dedicated to increasing the quality of teaching and learning about politics in higher education settings. Although designed for the college level, it is especially useful for teachers and advanced high school students as well because it contains many links to very rich and useful Internet sites appropriate for all levels.

  V VI X

Center for American Women and Politics

http://www.rci.rutgers.edu/~cawp

A program of the Eagleton Institute at Rutgers University, the center provides fact sheets on women in elected offices from Congress through state legislatures. It also provides information on women as candidates and historical information on the role of women in the political process in America.

 V VI X

Open Secrets: The Center for Responsive Politics

http://www.opensecrets.org

Open Secrets is an online source for data about money in politics. This site shows how money flows into political campaigns and provides analyses of who is contributing to whom and for what purposes. This is an interesting site for both teacher and student research.

 V VI X

British Broadcasting Corporation World Service (BBC)

http://www.bbc.co.uk/worldservice/index.shtml

Often, the most interesting perspective on one's own country comes from abroad. The BBC World Service home page provides news from the United States (and almost everywhere else) in English. It also provides a guide to local BBC programming in the United States.

 V VI IX X

POLITICAL PARTIES

Although clearly reflecting their own positions and agendas, political party web sites provide good samples of party platforms, campaign strategies, and unique stances on important issues.

 V VI X

Democratic National Committee

http://www.democrats.org

Republican National Committee

http://www.rnc.org

Reform Party

http://www.reformparty.org

NEWS MEDIA

Massive coverage of political campaigns, congressional and legislative actions, and court decisions is provided on virtually all television and radio news shows, in newspapers, and in news magazines. The web sites maintained by these organizations give up-to-the-minute reporting on critical issues in government. Be sure to check out the web sites for your local news media and add them to this list.

Television Sources

Colorful, highly interactive, and updated from minute to minute, these web sites are good places to begin student coverage of important campaigns.

C-Span

http://www.c-span.org/

ABC News

http://www.abcnews.go.com/sections/politics

Fox News

http://www.foxnews.com/politics/index.html

CBS News

http://www.cbsnews.com/sections/politics/main250.shtml

CNN Inside Politics

http://www.cnn.com/ALLPOLITICS

MSNBC

http://www.msnbc.com/news/politics_front.asp

Newspapers

Hundreds of newspapers cover thousands of local political stories every day. These four are noted for their national and international political coverage.

Chicago Tribune

http://www.chicagotribune.com

Los Angeles Times

http://www.latimes.com/news/politics

New York Times

http://www.nytimes.com/pages/politics/index.html

Washington Post

http://www.washingtonpost.com/wp-dyn/politics

Weekly News Magazines

News magazines provide feature stories on current political events, often going behind the scenes for in-depth coverage and analysis. The three largest news weeklies maintain excellent web sites with dozens of useful features.

Newsweek

http://www.newsweek.com

Time

http://www.pathfinder.com/time

U.S. News and World Report

http://www.usnews.com/

CHAPTER 7

Geography

In October 1994, the U.S. National Geography Standards were published in Washington, D.C. An extensive presentation of these 18 standards with lesson plans and activities is available from the National Geographic Society's web site Xpeditions, **http://www.nationalgeographic.com/xpeditions/standards/index.html.** This site should be the starting point for teachers who will teach geography.

National Geographic Society

http://www.nationalgeographic.com

This is a gateway web site that provides access to the world of geography. Xpeditions provides over 600 printable maps for use in the classroom and a variety of activities and information that would enhance geography education. It regularly offers special features on its Expeditions and Exhibits sections.

 I III IV

National Council for Geographic Education

http://www.ncge.org

In addition to council events and programs, under Activities one can progress through a tutorial that explains the approaches and ideas for the Six Geography Themes and Eighteen Standards of Geography. It is particularly valuable to a teacher unfamiliar with the standards.

 I III IX

United States Geological Survey

http://mapping.usgs.gov/

This site offers comprehensive lesson plans for different grade levels. The Land and People section includes global change and other contemporary topics. Information that allows integration of science and social studies is prevalent.

 I III IX

National Atlas of the United States

http://www.nationalatlas.gov

This site, also developed by the U.S. Geological Survey, creates an atlas of U.S. natural and social-cultural landscapes. Interactive multimedia maps aid in the visualization and comprehension of complex relationships among places, people, and environments. You will need to download the Shockwave plug-in, which is provided by the site.

 I III IX

Maps.com

http://www.maps.com/learn/

At Maps.com there are outline physical and political maps and globe images for the world and the United States that can be used as transparencies and as print images for students to complete. The games section and interactive map kit can be very effective with elementary and middle school instruction.

 III IX

Atlapedia Online

http://www.atlapedia.com

This site provides full-color maps and encyclopedia-type information that can be used in a variety of ways by both teachers and students. Facts, statistics, and maps can be accessed by country name or world region.

 I III IX

CIA World Factbook

http://www.cia.gov/cia/publications/factbook/

An up-to-date and factually accurate listing of data by country that is updated in real time. Includes categories such as maps, transportation, people, government, economy, communications, and transnational issues.

 I III IX

50 States and Capitals

http://www.50states.com

This site provides easy access to statistical and historical information for each of the 50 states of the union. Also included are the lyrics to state songs and their melodies, which can be heard with the Real Player software.

 III

Library of Congress American Memory Historical Collection

http://memory.loc.gov/ammem/gmdhtml/gmdhome.html

An array of historical and contemporary maps of North America can be accessed and used in history as well as geography classes.

 II III

Historical Maps at the University of Texas Library

http://www.lib.utexas.edu/maps/historical/index.html

This site has original resources, as well as links to other sites with historical maps, organized by historical periods and regions. This resource can be used for history or geography.

 II III IX

Explore the Globe Program

http://www.globe.gov/fsl/welcome.html

This site is ideal for elementary-level teachers who have a strong interest in active learning approaches. In addition to interactive activities for students, educators can access a Teacher's Guide, a Data Archive, and an Image Gallery.

 I III IV

Leonard's "Cam World"

http://www.leonardsworlds.com/camera.html

This travel-based site offers over 2,500 outdoor cameras in real time at locations around the world. Visitors can access travel information for cities and other locations.

 I III IV

Reprinted with permission of Richard Darsie.

Tales of Wonder

http://www.darsie.net/talesofwonder/

This is an excellent site for integration of literature into social studies geography curricula.

 I II IX

The Global Schoolhouse

http://www.gsn.org

This site provides advice on use of the Internet to connect with schools around the world and offers many projects that encourage global awareness.

 IX III

The Ancient World

http://julen.net/ancient/General_Resources

For teachers who aspire to integrate lessons about world history with geography, anthropology, and other disciplines, this site provides resources and background information.

 I II III IX

The Great Globe Gallery

http://hum.amu.edu.pl/~zbzw/glob/glob1.htm

This site has hundreds of images of the globe and information on global changes.

 III IX

Additional Geography Web Sites

National Weather Service

http://www.nws.noaa.gov/

Blank Maps of Countries and States

http://geography.about.com/cs/blankoutlinemaps/

Country Reports

http://www.countryreports.org

Epals Classroom Exchange

http://www.epals.com/home.html

Yale University Map Collection

http://www.library.yale.edu/MapColl/curious.html

Gateway to Geography Games

http://members.aol.com/bowermanb/games.html

Maps of Native American Nations
http://indy4.fdl.cc.mn.us/~isk/maps/mapmenu.html#buttons

Web Geological Time Machine
http://www.ucmp.berkeley.edu/help/timeform.html

How Far Is It?
http://www.indo.com/cgi-bin/dist

GIS Dictionary of Geography Terms
http://www.geo.ed.ac.uk/agidict/welcome.html

U.S. Census Bureau Data, 1790–1960
http://fisher.lib.virginia.edu/census

The Weather Channel
http://www.weather.com/

ETHNOLOGUE: Languages of the World
http://www.sil.org/ethnologue

6 Billion and Beyond
http://www.pbs.org/sixbillion/

A Solar/Terrestrial Tutorial
http://vortex.plymouth.edu/sun.html

Flags of the World
http://atlasgeo.span.ch/fotw/flags/iso3166.html (new address)

Economics and Geography Lessons for 32 Children's Books
http://www.mcps.k12.md.us/curriculum/socialstd/Econ_Geog.html

National Geographic's Map Matching
http://www.nationalgeographic.com/maps/

Awesome Library
http://www.awesomelibrary.org/Library/Materials_Search/Lesson_Plans/Social_
Studies.html

Florida Alliance's 100 Geography Lesson Plans

http://fga.freac.fsu.edu/lessonplans.html

See the USA: Webquest Simulation

http://www.esc20.net/etprojects/formats/webquests/friends/seeusa/index.html

Ellis Island Virtual Tour

http://capital.net/~alta/

CHAPTER 8

Economics

No aspect of the social studies touches our lives more directly than economics. Virtually every decision we make every day is affected in some way by economic forces. Fortunately, there are excellent resources for teachers who wish to incorporate this critical and engaging subject into their classes. Most of the web sites featured in this section include lesson plans and instructional materials for K–12 use. Others provide research data, interactive experiences for students, or online access to programs and projects sponsored by governments, educational institutions, businesses, or other agencies.

U.S. Treasury Department

http://www.treas.gov

Treasury's home page tells the story of the department with an illustrated history from its founding in 1789. The link to the Bureau of Engraving and Printing web site offers educational games, teacher resources, and a chat room where students can ask questions about money and how it is produced.

     II V VI VII X

Reprinted with permission of the National Council on Economic Education.

National Council on Economic Education

http://www.nationalcouncil.org

The National Council on Economic Education is a partnership of leaders in education, business, and labor devoted to helping youngsters function in a changing global economy. This is an especially rich source of information, teaching materials, and teacher training opportunities. The council also sponsors Economics America, a network of state councils and over 260 university-based centers for economic education. This site is a gateway to lessons, content materials, and other valuable web sites devoted to the teaching of economics and sound economic decision making by students at all levels of education. Among the many engaging resources are economic simulations, materials for students in grades K–12, and planning tools for teachers. The CyberTeach guide makes it easy for teachers to access web sites that support economics curricula. It includes information on basic web skills, provides examples of lessons that teach economic concepts, and gives step-by-step instructions on how to construct economics lessons using the Internet.

     VII IX

Reprinted with permission of Economic Education Web, Economics Department, University of Nebraska, Omaha.

Economic Education Web

http://ecedweb.unomaha.edu/home.htm

The Economic Education Web, or EcEdWeb, is sponsored by the University of Nebraska at Omaha's Center for Economic Education. This award-winning site offers comprehensive resources for teachers at all levels (K–college). Besides serving as a superb gateway to other economics education sites, EcEdWeb provides excellent materials of its own, including key economic concepts for students at all levels, descriptions of "evidence of student learning" that can be used to shape assessments, and thoughtful suggestions on using the Internet to teach economics concepts in K–12 school settings. The links to other web sites have been selected and reviewed for both quality of content and ease of use. This is an excellent place to start for teachers developing an economics curriculum in their own schools or for those who want to integrate economics content into other subject fields.

 VII IX

NetEc

http://netec.wustl.edu

Hosted by Washington University's Department of Economics, NetEc is an international academic effort to improve the communication of economics via electronic media. Two of its most useful subsections are WebEc, a hosted, searchable library of free economics resources on the Internet, and JokeEc, a vast collection of jokes about economics that serve as an excellent springboard for the teaching of basic economic concepts as well as some of its more subtle nuances. This award-winning site is a great source of background information for teachers who are interested in enriching their own understanding of economics and econometrics.

 VII IX

Federal Reserve Bank of San Francisco

http://www.frbsf.org/education/index.html

The Federal Reserve Bank is the central bank of the United States. The San Francisco branch provides teaching resources on its own site as well as links to other economics education sites across the Internet. The site supplies both student materials and lesson plans focusing on the history and development of monetary systems, simulations exploring supply and demand, and an "Ask Dr. Econ" feature, where students can get responses to specific questions about money and economics.

 VII IX

The Mint

http://www.themint.org

The Mint bills itself as an integrated web site for middle school and high school students, their teachers, and their parents and is provided by Northwestern

Mutual and the National Council on Economic Education. Focused on the individual and the economy, this site provides information on starting your own business, saving and investing, spending and consuming, budgeting, and your role in the economy. A special feature points out the financial rewards of completing college and helps students learn to exercise caution in making credit purchases. The site also provides access to Gazillionaire, an online, intergalactic investment and finance game.

VI IX

Reprinted with permission of The Development Education Program, World Bank Institute, World Bank.

The World Bank

http://www.worldbank.org/html/schools

Recently surrounded by controversy, the World Bank is a global effort to invest in those nations where the need is greatest. In addition to materials on the teaching of economics, the World Bank web site provides information on developing countries and regions, the big issues in the developing world, and solid economic data that can be used for research and instruction. Its stated mission to help cultivate empathy and respect for people in developing nations leads this site to help students experience poverty and the promise of economic growth through the eyes of children and adults in these nations.

 VII IX

The Stock Market Game

http://www.smg2000.org

The Stock Market Game was the first—and is still one of the best—large-scale simulations about how money and investing work to power a global economy. Over the course of 10 weeks, participants invest their hypothetical $100,000 in NASDAQ, AMEX, and NYSE stocks. They research stocks, study how the financial markets work, choose their portfolios, manage budgets, follow companies in the news, and make decisions on whether to buy, sell, or hold. They can compare their portfolios' performance to those of peers on a weekly basis. The Stock Market Game is a trademarked program of the Securities Industry Foundation for Economic Education (SIFEE) and is designed to promote understanding of how the stock market works and how individuals can invest in a market economy.

    VII IX

EconoLink from The Progress Report

http://www.progress.org/econolink

This gateway site is sponsored by The Progress Report, part of the Economic Justice Network. The site offers links to a number of interesting and provocative resources, many of which provide a view of economic behavior and policy that is quite different from capitalism and market economics. Students, journalists, activists, and program developers can all find material that challenges conventional wisdom and provides counterpoint to mainstream economic education sites.

  VII IX X

 Federal Citizen Information Center Pueblo, Colorado

Consumer Information Center

http://www.pueblo.gsa.gov

Provided by the Consumer Information Center of the U.S. General Services Administration (GSA), this site gives access to hundreds of product information resources and consumer guides on everything from buying a car to looking for a job. This is an excellent site for students engaged in research on popular products and informed buying.

  VII

U.S. Department of Commerce

http://www.commerce.gov

The Commerce Department is charged with promoting job growth, sustainable development, and improved economic opportunities for all citizens. Through the National Oceanic and Atmospheric Administration, it makes possible the weather reports heard every morning. It facilitates technology that Americans use in the workplace and at home every day. It supports the development, gathering, and transmitting of information essential to competitive business. It makes possible the diversity of companies and goods found in America's (and the world's) marketplaces. It supports environmental and economic health for the communities in which Americans live; and it conducts the constitutionally mandated decennial census, which is the basis of representative democracy. The department's web site is a gateway to all of these useful and informative resources, which support sound economics instruction.

 VI VII IX X

AskEric Lesson Plans

http://askeric.org/cgi-bin/lessons.cgi/Social_Studies/Economics

This very useful, teacher-friendly site provides lessons for all aspects of social studies. The economics section is especially good for teachers in grades 4–12. The lessons are all developed by practitioners for practitioners, so they are straightforward and workable. Most include all necessary materials.

 VI VII IX X

Escape from Knab

http://www.escapefromknab.com/land.html

In order to purchase the $10,000 ticket required to return to Earth, students must make good earning, investing, and savings decisions after finding themselves stranded on the planet Knab. Knabians are friendly enough, but slimy and foul-smelling. Naturally, kids love them—and this engaging game.

 VII IX

Teachers Resource Center

http://www.plan.ml.com/family/teachers

This site provides excellent resources for teachers on saving and investing. It also serves as a very helpful gateway to dozens of Internet resources on how the economy works, featuring recommended books that contain economic lessons for children of all ages.

     VI IX X

ThinkQuest Library: Business & Industry—Money, Economics and Finance

http://www.thinkquest.org/library/IC_index.html

This library of student-authored resources is a great place for students to begin their own research. It also provides excellent models for high-quality student work.

  VII IX X

Lemonade Stand

http://www.lemonadegame.com

This is a World Wide Web version of the classic computer game Lemonade Stand, with several differences. "High Game Scores" posted on the site allow students to compete with the best-performing kids from all over the nation.

 VII

Ubuyacar

http://www.mcli.dist.maricopa.edu/pbl/ubuystudent/index.html

This problem-based learning site from Maricopa (Arizona) Community College leads students through a productive problem-solving process on how to make good economic decisions, specifically, how to buy a car. This is a real hit with middle and high school kids.

 VII

Wall Street Research Network

http://www.wsrn.com

The Wall Street Research Network bills itself as having the "most comprehensive resources for investors on the Web." This wide-ranging site is especially useful for older students or as a teacher resource.

 VII IX X

AFL-CIO

http://www.aflcio.org/home.htm

Representing over 13 million workers, the largest U.S. labor union provides useful information on the history of the labor movement and a labor perspective on contemporary issues and the global economy.

 II V VII IX X

InvestSmart

http://stocksquest.thinkquest.org/10326/main.html

A Yahoo® Cool Site, InvestSmart reveals the secrets of smart stock investing. It provides a free stock market game and information on mutual funds trading for educators and individuals. The site offers investment lessons with convincing, real-life examples.

 VII IX

Economics and Geography Lessons for 32 Children's Books

http://www.mcps.k12.md.us/curriculum/socialstd/Econ_Geog.html

This teacher-friendly site from the Montgomery (Maryland) County Public Schools provides lessons for teaching economics content through 32 different children's books. Written by teachers, this site is very practical and triggers ideas for developing economics lessons around other children's books and young adult books as well.

 VII IX X

Additional Economics Web Sites

National Institute for Consumer Information
http://www.emich.edu/public/coe/nice

Social Security and You: Teachers Kit
http://www.ssa.gov/teacher/teacher.html

Resources for Economists on the Internet
http://rfe.wustl.edu/EconFAQ.html

World Wide Web Resources for Teaching and Learning Economics—ERIC Digest
http://www.ed.gov/databases/ERIC_Digests/ed424189.html

Bureau of Labor Statistics
http://stats.bls.gov

Classroom Lessons from Ayers Online
http://www.ayersonline.com/Toolbox/tool.htm

Current Value of Old Money
http://www.ex.ac.uk/~RDavies/arian/current/howmuch.html

Tax Policy
http://www.taxpolicy.com

Internal Revenue Service
http://www.irs.gov

CHAPTER 9

Anthropology, Sociology, and Psychology

Sociology and anthropology are closely aligned disciplines that examine human interactions. Sociology is focused on group processes, and anthropology centers on cultural change and diffusion. Psychology focuses on humans' behavior and thoughts as humans interact with stimuli in the environment. A number of web sites capture the far-ranging scope of these disciplines.

ANTHROPOLOGY AND SOCIOLOGY

American Anthropological Association

Reprinted with permission of the American Anthropological Association.

American Anthropological Association

http://www.aaanet.org/

This is the official site of the American Anthropological Association and provides access to brochures (i.e., *What Is Anthropology?*) as well as press releases on recent articles and papers published by the AAA. The site is broken down into several categories: Careers, Ethics, Government Affairs, Minority Issues in Anthropology, Press Relations, Publications, and Anthropology Resources on the Internet. This site is updated weekly and claims to be current on issues and concerns in the field of anthropology. There are in excess of 50 links on this site to other informative sites related to anthropology.

 I II IV V

UCSB Anthropology Web Site

http://www.anth.ucsb.edu/index.html

Although this web site was created for graduate students, it is an excellent reference source for teachers as well as students. It contains links to numerous web sites on any anthropology area and available software links as well. Another great feature is an online glossary of anthropological terms used in each subdiscipline in anthropology. It also contains an area devoted to anthropological projects, such as "digs" in various areas and reports on the progress in new developments. There is another area for information on famous anthropologists and their accomplishments.

 I II III IV

ArchNet

http://www.lib.uconn.edu/ArchNet

A well-organized, comprehensive anthropology site that includes links to over 119 museums, anthropology sites, and universities. This site excels in both its subject areas, ranging from Archaeometry to Method & Theory sections, and regional search capabilities. This search feature can locate any place on the globe and give you a list of all sites pertaining to this geographical area. This site is easily translated into several languages, a nice feature for bilingual students. Also included is a search engine by subject or area of interest, links to journals and other online publications, online site tours and software for mapping.

 I II III IV

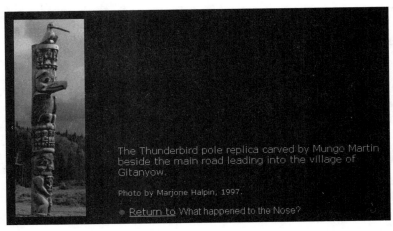

The Thunderbird pole replica carved by Mungo Martin beside the main road leading into the village of Gitanyow.

Photo by Marjorie Halpin, 1997.

● Return to What happened to the Nose?

Reprinted with permission of Dr. Marjorie M. Halpin.

Prelude to the Study of a Totem Pole

http://www.moa.ubc.ca/Virtual/Other/prelude2/start.html

This site is very informative on the history and meaning of totem poles. Visitors can find a bibliography of works discussing the art of totem poles. Throughout the site, specific anthropology terms are defined, making reading more understandable for newcomers. One portion of the site allows visitors to select particular sections of the pole to learn more about the story and also provides an opportunity to see how the pole would change if the story was told differently. Teachers can use this site to assign research projects on totem poles—how they originated, what the poles mean, and their significance to that culture. In addition, this site provides links to journals and museums.

 I II III IV

Anthropology Resources at the University of Kent

http://lucy.ukc.ac.uk/

This is a truly unique site that allows people to witness what anthropological fieldwork is like. The site features Stephon Lyon, a doctoral student from the University of Kent, who is doing research in Bhaloti, a village located in Northern Pakistan. Visitors to this web site can read Lyon's daily fieldnotes, as well as weekly updates and monthly reports. In addition, visitors can read stories and listen to music created by the villagers themselves. Lyon encourages people to send him comments about his research.

 I II IV V IX X

Smithsonian Institution Libraries, Anthropology on the Internet for K–12

http://www.sil.si.edu/SILPublications/Anthropology-K12

This site gives its visitors a broad review of anthropology with historical and current issues and research. Specific topics on the site include, but are not limited to, Archaeology, Social/Cultural Anthropology, Physical Anthropology, and Linguistics. There is a comprehensive Internet guide to resources about many different cultures—past and present—ranging from excavations and site/regional reports to concept and teaching sites. The site gives access to virtual exhibits, electronic publications, and career links. In addition, there are numerous illustrations and pictures of artifacts.

 I II III IV V IX X

Looking At Ourselves and Others

<u>Contents</u>

Peace Corps Global Education World Wise Schools

http://www.peacecorps.gov/wws/guides/looking/index.html

The goal of site, "Looking at Ourselves and Others," is to challenge "World Wise" students to become more conscious of the values they share with their families, friends, and communities. The site provides analytical tools that help combat stereotypical thinking and enhance cross-cultural communication. The teacher's guide is arranged by topic, including teacher background information, activity outlines, and student worksheets. Many activities are similar to those used to help prepare Peace Corps Volunteers for their cross-cultural experiences. The activities for each topic are further divided according to three suggested groupings: grades 3–5, 6–9, and 10–12. Each activity outline has at least six parts: an estimate of class time needed, materials, a statement of objectives, step-by-step procedures, debriefing exercises, and suggestions for extending the activity.

 I III IV V VI VII IX X

Roadsideamerica.com

http://www.roadsideamerica.com/

This is an excellent site in which the viewer is able to see many of America's strangest roadside attractions, unknown to many. The slogan of the site sums it up very well, "Your online guide to offbeat attractions." At this site, you are able to view the odd attractions in a state of your choice or follow a road trip, set up by the experts at this site, to see many of these great attractions.

 I IV V

Florida's Underwater Archaeological Preserves

http://www.dos.state.fl.us/dhr/bar/uap

This is a wonderful site that explores and discusses Florida's statewide system of underwater parks featuring shipwrecks and other historical underwater sites. This site shows pictures and descriptions of the six present parks, as well as others that are under development. Each archaeological site is open all year and free of charge.

    II IV

American Museum of Natural History

http://www.amnh.org/

This interactive site provides visitors with detailed information on natural history. Time lines, which could be useful in the classroom, provide specific information on periods dating back to the Devonian period and up to the Pleistocene period. Visitors to this site could also take a tour through numerous exhibitions in the museum, including one of the world's largest exhibits of dinosaur fossils. While visiting this site, one could also look up current events or witness a volcano explode.

     I II III IV IX

The University of Memphis Institute of Egyptian Art and Archaeology

http://www.memst.edu/egypt/main.html

This web site is dedicated to Ancient Egypt. Teachers and students can take a tour of different places in Egypt and see color photos of various attractions. For example, a student or teacher can take a tour of Giza and see photos of the pyramids and the Sphinx. People can see photos of different Egyptian artifacts as well. The site also has links to other Egyptian web sites, including one where teachers and students can learn about the different gods and their stories and myths. There is also a link to a site where students can learn about Egypt today.

   I II III

THE GALLUP ORGANIZATION
PRINCETON

Reprinted with permission of the Gallup Organization.

The Gallup Organization

http://www.gallup.com/

The Gallup Organization web site deals with current events. There are also articles about politics and current social issues affecting our society. Teachers and students can use this site to learn about current events, people's reaction to them, and issues affecting our world today.

   I III IV V VII VIII IX X

Additional Anthropology and Sociology Sites

Cultural Survival

http://www.culturalsurvival.org/home/index.cfm

World Game

http://www.worldgame.org/

Nacirema

http://www.beadsland.com/nacirema

Library of Congress American Folklife Center

http://lcweb.loc.gov/folklife/

World Health Organization

http://www.who.int/home-page/

MayaQuest

http://mayaquest.classroom.com/

Allyn and Bacon Sociology

http://www.abacon.com/sociology/soclinks/index.html

A Guide to Internet Resources in Anthropology

http://faculty.plattsburgh.edu/richard.robbins/legacy/anth_on_www.html#links

Critical Bibliography on North American Indians for K–12

http://www.nmnh.si.edu/anthro/outreach/Indbibl/index.html

The Margaret Mead Centennial 2001

http://www.mead2001.org/

Fieldwork: The Anthropologist in the Field

http://www.melanesia.org/fieldwork/tamakoshil/

CultureQuest

http://www.geocities.com/Athens/Oracle/6676/

Kinship and Social Organization

http://www.umanitoba.ca/anthropology/kintitle.html

MadSci Network

http://www.madsci.org

Anthropology in the News

http://www.tamu.edu/anthropology/news.html

Sociology: Chapter by Chapter

http://www.usi.edu/libarts/socio/chapter/chapter.htm

Oriental Institute

http://www-oi.uchicago.edu/OI/default.html

Worldwide Email Directory of Anthropologists

http://wings.buffalo.edu/WEDA

National Association for Humane and Environmental Education

http://www.nahee.org/

LSU Libraries—Anthropology Subject Guide

http://www.lib.lsu.edu/soc/anthro.html

Native Web

http://www.nativeweb.org

Western Connecticut State University Department of Social Studies

http://vax.wcsu.edu/socialsci/antres.html

A Sociological Tour Through Cyberspace

http://www.trinity.edu/~mkearl/

Erasing Native American Stereotypes

http://www.nmnh.si.edu/anthro/outreach/sterotyp.html

Rabbit in the Moon

http://www.halfmoon.org/

PSYCHOLOGY

The most "human" of all the social sciences, psychology is all about people, as individuals, in groups, and as a species with very unique characteristics and abilities. Students are usually fascinated by the study of psychology, largely because it has built-in relevance to their own lives. The sites described here are important gateways to this vast and engaging field.

The American Psychological Society Teaching Resources

http://psych.hanover.edu/aps/teaching.html

The American Psychological Society provides a gateway to dozens of useful sites and resources specifically for the teaching of psychology. It includes materials for general, behavioral, cognitive, health, forensic, and social psychology, as well as information on statistics, research methods, and other topics related to the field. This site is straightforward and helpful for teachers and more mature students.

   III IV V

Reprinted with the permission of the American Psychological Association.

American Psychological Association—for Kids

http://www.kidspsych.org/index1.html

Provided by the APA, this engaging site is all about "understanding ourselves and understanding each other." It includes entertaining games that challenge children to think in new and creative ways. For each activity, the site provides a list of theoretical and research publications that address the psychology of the task. Forget about the kids, adults will spend hours on this one.

 IV V

American Psychological Association

http://www.apa.org

The APA's site offers a "public" section that provides well-written materials on a number of contemporary psychological issues, such as mental health, applied behavior, or social problems. Designed for teachers of psychology in secondary schools, the TOPPS section of this site (**http://www.apa.org/ed/topsshomepage. html**) offers excellent resources for high school instructors and students. Their Help site (**http://helping.apa.org**) gives access to online assistance with real life problems.

 III IV V

Psychology Resources on the Internet

http://teachpsych.lemoyne.edu/teachpsych/div/teachpsychlinks.html

This site provides teachers with access to instructional materials in psychology and related fields. Sponsored by the Society for the Teaching of Psychology, it links directly to other specialist organizations as well as to other gateway sites.

 IV V

The Gateway

http://www.thegateway.org/

The Gateway to Educational Materials (GEM) project is an effort to provide teachers with quick and easy access to vast, uncataloged collections of educational materials on various federal, state, university, nonprofit, and commercial Internet sites. To access their section on Psychology, either type in "psychology" in the search field or click on the "Browse subjects" under "Search the Gateway," scroll to the social studies, and click on "psychology". The site is linked to some of the most important resources in the field and includes instructional units on conflict resolution, decision making, and generational conflicts, to name just a few.

 IV V

Resources in Psychology on the Internet

http://maple.lemoyne.edu/~hevern/psychref.html

Designed to support psychology instruction at Lemoyne College, this rich site is an excellent gateway to hundreds of other resources on the Internet. Available in either frames or text version, the site is extremely easy to navigate and very straightforward in its design. This is a great place to start planning a psychology course or to send students for independent research; it's a veritable one-stop resource.

 IV V

Classics in the History of Psychology

http://psychclassics.yorku.ca/

This fascinating resource was developed by Christopher Green from York University, Toronto, Canada. It provides full-text versions of the classics in the field, from the ancients to contemporary thinkers and scholars. This is a virtual textbook for a history of psychology course, and a great resource for students and teachers.

 IV V

Neuroscience for Kids

http://faculty.washington.edu/chudler/neurok.html

This highly interactive site leads students on an exploration of the nervous system. From playing synaptic tag to singing songs about the brain, teachers can access engaging activities, experiments, and new discoveries. This is a well-designed site.

 IV V

Additional Psychology Web Sites

American Psychological Association: National High School Psychology Standards

http://www.apa.org/ed/natlstandards.html

Discovering Psychology

http://www.learner.org/discoveringpsychology/index.html

The University of Chicago: Student Counseling Virtual Pamphlet Collection

http://counseling.uchicago.edu/vpc/

Teachers of Psychology in Secondary Schools (TOPSS)

http://www.apa.org/ed/topsshomepage.html

Pfizer Brain: The World Inside Your Head

http://www.pfizer.com/brain/etour1.html

CHAPTER 10

Teaching About Controversial Issues, Tolerance, and Equity

Social studies, more than any other subject taught in schools, requires the teacher to diplomatically engage students in discussions that deal with highly personal and controversial public issues. The range of controversial issues in social studies that might be part of a classroom experience is potentially infinite. Intolerance in the form of racism, sexism, classism, and discrimination rejects diversity and stifles equity. Conversely, when differences are celebrated for bringing richness to interactions, changes leading toward social justice can be initiated.

The following sites explore links that can foster tolerance and cooperation. They can be helpful not only for teachers and students, but for parents as well. However, the special challenge imposed on social studies teachers requires a robust understanding of issues and a willingness to forge and maintain a democratic classroom. The following resources provide background information and suggested teaching methods on a number of controversial topics.

Reprinted with permission of Public Agenda Online.

Public Agenda Online

http://www.publicagenda.org

This site is an up-to-date resource for information on a variety of topics, from abortion to welfare. Each section contains an overview of the issue, fact files, ideas on how to frame the debate, unique statistics, graphs, and so on.

Professional Cartoonists Index

http://cagle.slate.msn.com/teacher/

Cartoons are an excellent way to introduce a current event that may be controversial. As an accepted form of social commentary, they provide powerful visuals that aid in the comprehension of multiple perspectives. This site includes cartoons from nearly 100 daily newspapers.

Human Rights Watch

http://www.hrw.org

This site maintains updated information from around the world on human rights abuses. It includes breaking news, background information, ongoing events, and commentaries on regional abuses.

The Hate Directory

http://www.bcpl.lib.md.us/~rfrankli/hatedir.htm

This site provides visitors with a comprehensive list of hate groups on the Internet. Teachers may also find it useful as a reference or as a historical document, as defunct hate web sites are included with the list of active hate sites. In addition, this site provides a directory of links to other web pages that combat hate on the Internet, such as HateWatch, the Anti-Defamation League, and Cyberwatch.

HateWatch@Tolerance.org

http://www.hatewatch.org

This project provides a public forum for those interested in exchanging views on hate crimes and prejudice. The catalog of current web-based hate groups allows visitors to view the sites that are being used to proliferate hate. HateWatch provides current news on evolving hate issues and gives assistance to hate crime victims. This site also includes video presentations, a web-based radio show, and online interviews with those advocating and condemning hate crimes.

Reprinted with permission of the Anti-Defamation League.

Anti-Defamation League (ADL)

http://www.adl.org

The ADL site allows visitors to be informed about issues of prejudice and discrimination by providing news on international affairs, legislation, and domestic events. Special topics, such as the Nation of Islam, terrorism on the Internet, and school vouchers, are displayed with commentaries and news updates related to these issues. Teachers are provided with lesson plans, videos, and books on prejudice and communication among diverse groups. There are helpful ideas for celebrating holidays in a way that is democratic. This site also allows parents to find ideas and sources to support their communication with their children on issues of hate crimes and discrimination.

UNICEF Voices of Youth

http://www.unicef.org/voy

UNICEF has organized this site into three general areas that address global issues on children's rights: The Meeting Place, The Learning Place, and The Teacher's Place. The Meeting Place is where students can go to share ideas with others around the world on issues concerning human rights. The Learning Place provides students with activities, such as quizzes on current children's rights topics, online classrooms, and suggestions for starting youth groups. Some of the activities might focus on areas like child labor, HIV/AIDS, or different cultural treatment toward girls. The Teacher's Place is where teachers are able to discuss educational and global issues with other teachers, plus find lesson plans, assignments, and links to other discussion groups.

Amnesty International (AI)

http://www.amnesty.org.uk

Amnesty International has developed this site in order for visitors to become involved in and informed about global human rights. The library contains reports on international campaigns against oppressive governments that are violating the International Declaration of Human Rights. Teacher resources are available, with videos of different amnesty campaigns, software packages, bibliographies of useful publications, and lesson plans integrating human rights awareness. Students are given resources in order to take action with letter-writing campaigns, assemblies, starting a youth group, and individual action packs. AI also provides the most recent press releases, articles, and updates on individual cases that have been the focus of a particular campaign by students and/or members of Amnesty International.

American Civil Rights Review

http://webusers.anet-stl.com/~civil/index.html

This site provides the most current news on racism, civil rights, hate crimes, and discrimination. Various sources and web sites are available to provide the complete perspective of civil rights issues through sound bytes, articles, and links. This site will add fire to any discussion by allowing visitors access to other web sites that promote conspiracy theories, white rights, circus freak rights, international genocide, immigration issues, and many more.

Cybrary of the Holocaust

http://www.remember.org

This site contains many resources and educational activities in order that the memories of the Holocaust will not be forgotten by today's students. This cybrary provides teachers with various lesson plans ranging from topics on Jewish history to the Nazis' "Final Solution." Teachers may also meet other educators online through this site to share ideas, exchange lesson plans, and identify new books available on the topic. The images of the Holocaust are kept alive with a virtual tour of Auschwitz, various photo galleries, personal stories from survivors, and music that resulted from the events of World War II. This site also presents ways in which families of victims and survivors can find out the details and chronology of their family members' plight in the death camps. Students will be able to see art and poetry created by other students who have learned about the Holocaust.

United Nations CyberSchoolBus Human Rights in Action

http://www0.un.org/cyberschoolbus/humanrights/index.asp

This site was developed in order for students to gain a sense of themselves by taking action against human rights abuse. Students can understand the International

Declaration of Human Rights through an interactive process that provides activities, discussion topics, terminology and text explanations, and Q-and-A sessions with experts on the declaration. Teachers are encouraged to put their students into action with various lesson plans and projects. In addition, students and teachers can share their ideas of action with others through online discussion groups. Other helpful links on this site educate visitors with a human rights bibliography, vocabulary builder, facts and figures, and personal stories of human rights abuses.

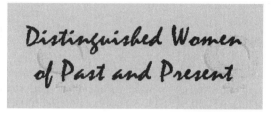

Reprinted with permission of Danuta Bois.

Distinguished Women of Past and Present

http://www.DistinguishedWomen.com

Visitors to this site can find biographical profiles of women of the past and present who have become distinguished in literature, education, science, politics, civil rights, art, entertainment, and other fields. Current updates of distinguished women in the news and the titles of recommended books written by or about women are also available on this site. Links to other web pages such as The Most Powerful Women in the World, Early Women Masters of the East and West, 100 Celebrated Chinese Women, and the Ecofeminism Homepage are included. The Black History Month feature allows a search by field for profiles of distinguished African-American women and also provides resourceful links to sites of African-American history.

TAP Junior

http://www.cs.yale.edu/~tap/tap-junior.html

TAP Junior—a division of Tapping Internet Resources—is dedicated to promoting the understanding of science, math, and technology for girls K–12. This site contains many links to organizations, activities, and other web sites that allow girls to become more adept at computing skills. For example, there are postings for computer camps, presentations of national education programs for promoting computer literacy, interactive museum tours, examples of computer games specifically made for girls, and many others. Educators and parents may find resources that promote understanding of math and science for students 9–12. There are also links for girls to share ideas, view current news of world events and entertainment, and find activities that expand their interest in the computing field. This site is also open to submissions and feedback to increase its development into a valuable resource.

Reprinted with permission of WEEA Equity Resource Center, EDC.

Women's Educational Equity Act (WEEA) Equity Resource Center

http://www.edc.org/WomensEquity

The Women's Educational Equity Act (WEEA) Equity Resource Center promotes awareness of gender equity among men and women in learning, developing, and achieving in society. Teachers can find lesson plans on gender equity legislation, sexual harassment issues, and distinguished women in history. *WEEA Digest* is available online to provide educators with current discussions on educational theory and field-based perspectives. There also are links to fun sites for girls, feminist sites, and online courses to engage middle school girls in math and science. E-mail discussions on equity issues are accessible, and information is provided for undergraduate women who want to become involved in gender equity issues on campus. Submission of gender equity materials, such as curricula or textbooks, to be evaluated by the WEEA expert panel, is encouraged.

Anti-Racist Action (Toronto)

http://www.web.apc.org/~ara/who/intro.htm

The Anti-Racist Action web site was designed to inform people about racism through presentations and demonstrations concerning antifascism and antiracism. The newsletter, called "On the Prowl," is filled with a variety of articles on racism, sexism, fascism, and other discriminatory practices. Teachers can use this newsletter to inform their students about racism and how it still exists today. Teachers can also get various ideas from this newsletter (e.g., students can find articles on hate crimes and design their own newsletters for other students to read). This web site also offers audio on works this group has done.

Fighting Hate Across the Nation

http://www.civilrights.org/

This web site is filled with a vast amount of information regarding intolerance. Visitors are provided with a definition of hate, statutes, laws, and so on. Real stories of people who have been affected by hate crimes are also included. Students can use this web site to write papers or get information and statistics on these ethical issues. The Anti-Hate Resource Center is linked with other web sites, Cyberwatch, HateWatch, and the Anti-Defamation League.

Simon Wiesenthal Center

http://www.wiesenthal.com/

The Simon Wiesenthal Center web page is an interactive site that allows visitors to explore many different avenues, such as virtual exhibits, special collections, and teacher resources. The Wiesenthal Center deals with the effects of racism. The multimedia library allows users to examine different types of information. Links to sites that facilitate access to historical documents are also provided.

Teaching Tolerance

http://www.splcenter.org/

The Southern Poverty Law Center web page on Teaching Tolerance addresses the efforts being made to help teach tolerance in the classroom. There are links attached to the site that give helpful information and resources for teachers as well as students on teaching tolerance of all races and other issues facing young people today.

Social Studies School Service

http://www.socialstudies.com/holo.html

This web site provides many resources in support of a social studies curriculum unit on the subject of the Holocaust. Teachers can find videos of contemporary films, CD–ROMs for Internet lessons, and many other media resources for the classroom. Samples from lesson plan books are provided to give educators some actual projects that are being used to present different perspectives. For example, projects are extracted from a unit plan based solely on the diaries of Anne Frank. Also helpful is a breakdown of what resources are appropriate for each grade level. Many links are provided, ranging from history tutorials to online museums.

WomenWatch

http://www.un.org./womenwatch

WomenWatch is a site dedicated to educating visitors on women's issues of advancement and empowerment. This site provides access to the global community of women who are working toward equity in areas of legislation, employment, and social status. Resources and links to women's organizations and conferences are provided in order to display the global organization of gender equity efforts.

Statistical and comparative trends are also displayed in the areas of women's employment, literacy, education, and income. Updates on current news and events focusing on women's rights are also available, with links to other gender equity sites and resources.

Women of Achievement and Hertory

http://www.undelete.org

The Women's Internet Information Network contains over 20,000 biographies of past and present accomplished women. In addition, this site has pictorial archives of photographs, prints, engravings, documents, and statues that exhibit the influence of women through different eras. Visitors to this site can also click on any day of the year to see what women accomplished on that day in history. This site contains links to organizations that fight for gender equity and provides a newsletter to present information on what is happening to women around the world.

All One Heart, "Diversity Tolerance Education"

http://www.alloneheart.com

This is a positive and inspiring web site for young adults and adults to explore. This site discusses issues regarding tolerance of all races and genders. One of the subject areas, Heart Burn, gives recent quotes by well-known people that include racially insensitive comments. This site also has an interactive message board to discuss hot topics and issues regarding discrimination, without promoting religious "recruitments."

Crosspoint Anti-Racism

http://www.magenta.nl/crosspoint

This site is extremely useful for students, teachers, and parents alike. It gives over a thousand different links to over a hundred countries to view topics concerning anti-racism. Viewers of this site can select a country to view topics, or they can select a subject area like "women," "human rights," or "Jewish resources." It also gives direct connections to many different search engines, which can be extremely helpful when searching different topic areas online. There is also a place to share comments and ideas on anti-racism.

National Organization for Women (NOW)

http://www.now.org

NOW is the largest feminist organization in the United States, with over 500,000 members. Through its web site, users can learn about resources, legislation, and actions used to fight gender inequalities. Some key issues that are discussed on this site include abortion, violence against women, and women in the military. Also located on the web site is the NOW newsline, where members write up-to-date news articles regarding world trends and developments and how NOW relates to and is involved with these events.

Stop the Hate

http://www.stopthehate.org

This web site is a Student Civil Rights Project that focuses on awareness and prevention of hate crimes. Teachers and students may find it useful as a resource in dealing with hate crimes and in deciding what hate crimes are taking place in their schools. The site also allows visitors to report hate crimes online so that they can help victims locate local assistance.

African American History

http://historicaltextarchive.com/sections.php?op=listarticles&secid=8

This African-American history site offers visitors a variety of topics and information regarding African Americans. This site allows people to view topics such as slavery, the military, and state and local history as well as bibliographies that deal with African Americans. It also provides information on African history in Canada. In addition, this site provides visitors with several links, including the Black History Museum.

A Teacher's Guide to the Holocaust

http://fcit.coedu.usf.edu/holocaust/default.htm

This guide provides a multitude of information to teachers about the Holocaust. The site includes activities and resources for students and teachers. This Holocaust site provides a time line as well as topics that describe people and the arts during this horrific time in history. Photographs and real-life stories of Jews are also displayed on this web site.

Victims of Child Abuse Laws—New York

http://www.vocalny.org/

This site is dedicated to providing information about child abuse laws. It includes articles about abused children who need help. It also provides other links to similar web sites. A list of books for education about child abuse is available. And, there is also advice for people who have been wrongly accused of child abuse. If additional information is needed, the user need only click on the provided link, and additional information will be sent.

American Professional Society on the Abuse of Children (APSAC)

http://www.apsac.org

This group is dedicated to training the professionals that deal with child abuse. It offers a variety of resources, including training sessions. Users can access the guidelines and publications generated by this group, including the handbook created by APSAC. Also, the site lists the legislation that the group currently advocates. Users have the option of joining the organization.

Prevent Child Abuse America (PCAA)

http://www.preventchildabuse.org

The PCAA site lets users read about the organization and its mission. In addition, the site lists resources for children, including hotline numbers and articles, such as "When Parents Drink Too Much." Also available are resources and information for parents. In addition to the resources generated by this organization, other resources, information, and links are available to users. Publications by the PCAA are available, and an opportunity to join this group is provided.

Commission for Racial Equality

http://www.cre.gov.uk/index.html

This organization promotes equality in all facets of life. The site provides information on the law and how it affects people against racism. It gives a complete background of the commission and its activities in the community. Information about discrimination and harassment is provided as well as human rights involved in these issues. The commission also provides support in certain discrimination cases and resources for education.

Anger Management Workshop—For Teachers & Professionals

http://www.angermgmt.com/workshop.html

This site is great for teachers, administrators, and parents who want to learn strategies for coping with a child's anger. It offers a workshop on how to manage a child's anger and even your own. Recommended readings and ordering sources are provided. This site also includes a table of contents area to check out different books, audiotapes, counseling, and a message board to answer any questions.

Visions, Inc.—Educational Services

http://www.visions-inc.com/serv07.htm

This is a valuable site because it increases one's knowledge on how to educate schools about racism, sexism, and intolerance in today's society. This site is a great tool for teachers who want to develop a classroom and curriculum that are free of discrimination. A list of key benefits and a contact site on how to receive free literature about this ever-growing problem are included. This site also offers a special training session to inform groups such as library staff, student groups, and advisors on how to be aware of and deal with these conflicts in school.

Beyond Prejudice

http://www.eburg.com/beyond.prejudice

Beyond Prejudice provides a multimedia guide on how to identify and change prejudice. This site provides materials that any teacher will find useful in the classroom, such as videotapes and printed material. It is also a great way for administrators to train their staff on becoming aware of prejudice in their classrooms. A table of contents accompanies this site. Some of the areas that it highlights are links to other related web pages, a quiz on prejudiced behavior, and a section on frequently asked questions.

Erasing Native American Stereotypes

http://www.nmnh.si.edu/anthro/outreach/sterotyp.html

Erasing Native American Stereotypes is located at the Smithsonian Institution's Anthropology Outreach Office web site. This site offers teachers advice on how to accurately present and study American Indian cultures—an excellent and recommended starting point for teachers as they begin to create and prepare lessons.

Center for Democratic Renewal (CDR)

http://www.publiceye.org/

Originally known as the National Anti-Klan Network, the Center for Democratic Renewal is a network of civil rights activists and organizations. It was founded as a multiracial organization in 1979 in response to racist violence and Klan activity. Today the CDR works to promote its vision of a democratic and diverse society free of racism and bigotry. Through programs of research, public education, and community organizing, the CDR has expanded its vision to many communities across the country, helping to combat racism and all forms of bias.

Searchlight Association

http://www.s-light.demon.co.uk/index.html

The Searchlight Association is an organization dedicated to the fight against racism and prejudice. It was formed in London in 1962 as a response to a resurgence of violent neo-Nazi activities. *Searchlight,* as a publication, has appeared as a monthly magazine since 1975 and is now read all over the world. Each year its members and staff speak at more than 200 schools, colleges, and conferences about the dangers of racism. The Searchlight Educational Trust was established to distribute educational materials to youth workers, teachers, and community leaders with the aim of enabling them to tackle racism and hatred.

Artists Against Racism

http://aar.vrx.net

This site provides resources for both teachers who are teaching about racism and students who are researching this topic. It provides up-to-date press releases, along with ideas on how to fight racism. In addition, teachers can use this web site to find quotes by many different artists whom students admire. These quotes can lead to classroom discussions about racism and the effects that it has on people's lives. Teachers may also use this site for finding videos and special projects that can be used in the classroom.

Combating Racism and Intolerance

http://www.coe.int/t/E/human_rights/ecri/

This site provides visitors with a wide range of information. This list extends from international legal texts, to initiatives in education, to a listing of agencies that are currently active in the fight against racism. For teachers, there are videos and graphics that can be used in lesson plans dealing with racism and intolerance. This site also allows both teachers and students to exchange information while critiquing and commenting on fellow users' ideas. Not only does this site give useful information on racism and intolerance, but it also shares examples of the current way of approaching racial problems.

Holocaust History Project

http://www.holocaust-history.org

This web site provides educators as well as students interested in the Holocaust with free archives of documents and essays. Also included in this site are essays by and opinions of those who believe that the Holocaust never happened. Teachers will find the background information useful in sparking discussion of different viewpoints of the Holocaust, including those of racists. This site also allows visitors to ask questions ranging from anti-Semitic influences to the children of the Holocaust. If the answer is not readily available, they will find it for you. Also available at this site are recordings and photographs dating back to World War II.

Lest We Forget—The Untold History of America

http://www.coax.net/people/LWF

A site dedicated to the accomplishments of African Americans, women, and Native Americans throughout the history of the United States. It contains a multitude of links, such as Writing Women into History, African Americans in the Revolutionary War Through the Vietnam War, Buffalo Soldiers, and Native American History and Culture. The links emphasize that history can be shown in various perspectives and that traditionally we have not received the full picture. The fact that these individuals' contributions have been overtly left out of textbooks is itself a lesson in racism and sexism.

International Education and Resource Network

http://www.iearn.org

Can we live in peace and coexistence with the rest of the world? This site provides an interactive tool to teach children from elementary to high school. There are various projects, such as Folk Games, Global Art and Music, and Laws of Life, that they can tackle with the interaction of other classrooms around the world. The result is that they find out that we are more alike than different from others and that young people can contribute for the good of our planet.

No Hate

http://www.muohio.edu/nohate

This site explains the importance of speaking up against hate. The motto that best describes that is "silence is acceptance, speak loudly." This anti-hate site makes a communitywide effort to stop hate crimes. This site gives you the information you need to take steps against hate crimes. It can be used for middle and high school classes.

SEPTEMBER 11 WEB RESOURCES

ABA Dialogue on Freedom

http://www.dialogueonfreedom.org

ABC News

http://abcnews.go.com/

AllKidsGrieve.org

http://www.allkidsgrieve.org

America-Mideast Educational and Training Services, Inc.

http://www.amideast.org

American Academy of Child & Adolescent Psychiatry

http://www.aacap.org/

American Academy of Pediatrics (AAP)

http://www.aap.org/advocacy/releases/disastercomm.htm

American-Arab Anti-Discrimination Committee (ADC)

http://www.adc.org

American Counseling Association

http://www.counseling.org/

American Psychological Association

http://helping.apa.org/daily/terrorism.html

American School Counselor Association

http://www.awaironline.org/

Arab American Institute

http://www.aaiusa.org

Association for Supervision and Curriculum Development

http://www.ascd.org/educationnews/resources.html

Bill of Rights Institute

http://www.billofrightsinstitute.org/pdf/911complete.pdf

Cable in the Classroom Taking Charge of Your TV in Troubled Times

http://www.ciconline.org/uploads/ML2News.pdf

CBS News

http://www.cbsnews.com

ChildTrauma Academy

http://www.ChildTrauma.org

CNN

http://www.cnn.com
http://www.cnn.com/2001/COMMUNITY/09/13/marans/index.html

Connect for Kids

http://www.connectforkids.org/resources3139/resources_show.htm?attrib_id=
6279&doc_id=82637

Constitutional Rights Foundation

http://www.crf-usa.org/Sept11/Sept11_home.html
http://www.crf-usa.org/terror/America%20Responds%20to%20Terrorism.htm

Council on American Islamic Relations (CAIR)

http://www.cair-net.org

Council on Islamic Education

http://www.cie.org

District of Columbia Public School System—Talking to Public School Students About Disasters

http://www.k12.dc.us/

Dougy Center for Grieving Children

http://www.grievingchild.org/

Educators for Social Responsibility

http://www.esrnational.org/

Emergency Services & Disaster Relief Branch, Center for Mental Health

http://www.mentalhealth.org/cmhs/emergencyservices/

ERIC Clearinghouse for Science, Mathematics, and Environmental Education Anthrax Information for Educators

http://www.ericse.org/anthrax.html

ERIC Clearinghouse for Social Studies/Social Science Education (ERIC/ChESS)

http://www.indiana.edu/~ssdc/91101.htm

Federal Emergency Management Agency (FEMA)

http://www.fema.gov/

Federal Emergency Management Agency FEMA for Kids

http://www.fema.gov/kids/

Fordam Foundation

http://www.edexcellence.net/Sept11/September11.html

Future of Children

http://www.futureofchildren.org/

George Mason University Psychological First Aid Kit

http://www.gmu.edu/departments/psychology

Network for Good

http://www.networkforgood.org/

Hospice Net

http://www.hospicenet.org/html/talking.html

Internet Education Foundation

http://www.neted.org/911/

Jane's Information Group

http://www.janes.com/index.shtml

KidsHealth

http://www.kidshealth.org/misc_pages/P_squarebanner.html

Liberty Unites

http://www.libertyunites.org/

Library of Congress

http://september11.archive.org/

Lightspan Partners

http://www.lightspan.com/portal/anationaltragedy.htm

Massachusetts General Hospital Responds

http://www.mgh.harvard.edu/DEPTS/pubaffairs/Issues/2001disaster.htm

Mr. Rogers

http://pbskids.org/rogers/parents/sept11a.htm

National Association for the Education of Young Children

http://www.naeyc.org/resources/eyly/1998/22.htm

National Association of School Psychologists

http://www.nasponline.org

National Center for Children Exposed to Violence (NCCEV)

http://www.nccev.org/

National Center for Post-Traumatic Stress Disorder

http://www.ncptsd.org/what_is_new.html

National Education Association—Crisis Communications Guide and Toolkit

http://www.nea.org/crisis

National Institute of Mental Health Helping Children & Adolescents Cope with Violence & Disasters

http://www.nimh.nih.gov/publicat/violence.cfm

National Institute of Mental Health Post-Traumatic Stress Disorder (PTSD), Trauma, Disasters, & Violence

http://www.nimh.nih.gov/anxiety/ptsdmenu.cfm

National Council for the Social Studies Teaching About Tragedy— Resources for Teachers and the Media

http://www.socialstudies.org/

National Mental Health Association

http://www.nmha.org/reassurance/children.cfm

National PTA

http://www.pta.org/parentinvolvement/tragedy/

National School Safety and Security Services

http://www.schoolsecurity.org/terrorist_response.html

National Victim's Assistance Organization

http://www.try-nova.org

New York University's Child Study Center

http://www.aboutourkids.org

North Carolina State's Cooperative Extension Services

http://www.ces.ncsu.edu/depts/fcs/humandev/disas3.html

Ohio Commission on Dispute Resolution and Conflict Management

http://www.state.oh.us/cdr/schools/trauma/tentips.htm

PBS: America Responds: Coverage of Events of Tuesday, September 11, 2001—Classroom Resources

http://www.pbs.org/americaresponds/educators.html

PBS 9-11: Looking Back . . . Moving Forward

http://www.pbs.org/inthemix/shows/show_9-11.html

PEW Research Center

http://www.pewinternet.org/reports/toc.asp?Report=69
http://www.pewinternet.org/reports/toc.asp?Report=46

Purdue Extension: Terrorism and Children

http://www.ces.purdue.edu/terrorism/children/index.html

Scholastic Inc.—America Unites

http://teacher.scholastic.com/professional/breaking_news/america_unites.htm

Sesame Workshop Education and Research Division

http://www.sesameworkshop.org/parents/advice/article/0,4125,49560,00.html#1

Social Science Research Council on 9/11

http://www.ssrc.org/sept11/

Time for Kids

http://www.timeforkids.com/TFK/

Tolerance.org—a Project of the Southern Poverty Law Center

http://www.tolerance.org

UCLA's School Mental Health Project

http://smhp.psych.ucla.edu/

University of Louisville Peace & Justice Committee
http://complicity.english.louisville.edu/peace/

University of Virginia Youth Violence Project
http://youthviolence.edschool.virginia.edu/

U.S. Department of Education
http://www.ed.gov/inits/september11/index.html

U.S. Department of Education—Religious Expression in Public Schools
http://www.ed.gov/Speeches/08-1995/religion.html

U.S. Government Information & Resources in Response to September 11th Events
http://www.firstgov.gov/Topics/Usgresponse.shtml

Wadsworth Publishing Company—Terrorism: An Interdisciplinary Perspective
http://www.wadsworth.com/sociology_d/

White House
http://www.whitehouse.gov/response/

Zero to Three
http://www.zerotothree.org/ztt_imh.html

CHAPTER 11

Teaching in a Pluralistic Society

Schools reflect society and attempt to provide all members of the American community an opportunity to succeed. Mainstreaming, latchkey children, immigration, economic differences, and technological changes present new challenges to teachers. The following resources will assist teachers in their aspirations to teach all the students found in a contemporary school setting.

LEARNING STYLES AND MULTIPLE INTELLIGENCES

It has long been recognized that students have different ways of learning, and they often have a preferred mode of learning that is more developed than alternative forms. Moreover, students may differ in their preferences for learning environments or conditions. In order to meet the variety of instructional needs of students, multiple intelligences (MI) theory has focused on teaching using diverse lessons that call on many types of intelligence. The following sites expand on strategies for addressing multiple intelligence theory and learning styles in order to increase the success of more students in the classroom.

Multiple Intelligences and Learning Styles

http://pdonline.ascd.org/pd_demo/table_c.cfm?SID=24

This online course introduces students to the theory of multiple intelligences. The site includes interactive lessons that have been specially designed for web-based training. Each lesson is supplemented with extensive reading material and access to discussion groups. This site also provides a stepping stone for more in-depth study on the effects that the different learning styles have on the classroom setting.

Multiple Intelligences

http://uwsp.edu/education/lwilson/LEARNING/index.htm

This site offers a brief introduction to Howard Gardner's multiple intelligences theory. It may be of particular interest to teachers as it provides information for practical application in the classroom. For each of the intelligences, an explanation is given, followed by behavioral indicators and suggested learning activities that teachers can use to implement multiple intelligences. Information is also provided as to the benefit of properly implementing MI.

The Key Learning Community

http://www.ips.k12.in.us/mskey

The Key School, located in Indianapolis, is the longest running school based on the theory of multiple intelligences. This site provides an interesting look inside a school that was created on the principles of Howard Gardner's theory. The curriculum is interdisciplinary, utilizes a multicultural approach, and incorporates technology. In addition to this exciting alternative to traditional education, the Key School presents the Key School Institute each summer to share the educational innovations of the school with participants from around the world.

"I think . . . therefore . . . M.I.!"

http://surfaquarium.com/intelligences.htm

This web site contains many links that exercise multiple intelligences. The site's creator has collected several viewpoints on Dr. Howard Gardner's Theory of Multiple Intelligences, one of which is a candid interview with Gardner. There also are links to great thinkers and visionaries, including Mother Theresa, Albert Einstein, and Mark Twain.

Teaching to the Seven Multiple Intelligences

http://www.mitest.com/

This web site provides a definition of multiple intelligences. It also presents an overview of research with accompanying graphics. Multiple intelligences information is broken down into age groups, and tests are included for adults, youth, and children. This site also presents lesson plans to use in mathematics, social science, social studies, and art units. At the end of the web site, there are links to other sites for multiple intelligences.

Multiple Intelligences

http://www.teachers.ash.org.au/teachereduc/indexTE.html

This site presents J. P. Guilford's and Howard Gardner's approaches to multiple intelligences. Ideas are included to help teachers utilize multiple modes of instruction and various forms of assessment to accommodate the various needs of their students. Web links related to multiple intelligences are provided.

NativeNet

http://nativenet.uthscsa.edu/archive/ne/96b/0013.html

NativeNet is a different kind of learning styles resource. On this particular site teachers will find an informative question and answer format on how teachers of Native American children can be better prepared and more knowledgeable on how their students learn. Comments from the respondents, many of whom are Native Americans themselves, are candid and offer much insight on unique situations teachers face in working within Native American cultures. Information in many cases is applicable to any classroom.

Education World

http://www.education-world.com/a_curr/curr054.shtml

This web site defines multiple intelligence and the eight different kinds of intelligences discussed in *Frames of Minds* by Howard Gardner. Suggestions for implementing Gardner's theory in the classroom are described. Education World also has a section guide that enables the visitor to view other subjects, including science, special education, and parent issues. Teachers are provided with lesson ideas and books that can be used in education.

Multiple Intelligence

http://www.ez2bsaved.com/Multiple_Intelligences/index-mi.htm

This site offers a comprehensive listing of links to sites on multiple intelligences, with background information and teaching strategies. Moreover, an index is provided that includes articles, checklists, and tests that are available online.

Family Education Network: Learning Styles

http://www.familyeducation.com

This site provides visitors with a definition of the eight multiple intelligences. It also provides tips for teachers and parents to help children help themselves. Articles and quizzes here pinpoint which learning style a child favors. Resource links can also help expand understanding of multiple intelligences and learning styles of students from preschool through high school and beyond.

Westmark School—Learning Styles

http://www.westmark.pvt.k12.ca.us/reading.html

This site provides an overview of the eight multiple intelligences, along with a list of behavior traits accompanying each intelligence. Through conversations with

Howard Gardner, it also includes teaching tips for multiple intelligences. Resource links are provided for learning styles, brain development, assistive technology, and learning differences.

Multiple Intelligences and Learning Styles

http://www.bham.wednet.edu/studentgal/onlinesearch/oldonline/mod9.htm

This site is about multiple intelligences and learning styles. It provides several informative sections on topics such as developing higher-order thinking skills, a rationale for using rock and roll in the classroom, and multiple intelligences lesson ideas. The site entertains the thought that exploration of the Internet supports a variety of learning styles and multiple intelligences. Links from the site provide more in-depth information on each of the previously mentioned subtopics.

MI—The Theory

http://www.ibiblio.org/edweb/edref.mi.th.html

This site gives a simple, yet informative, explanation of the traditional intelligence theories. It introduces Howard Gardner and his ideas on the intelligences. It also includes his most recent research. There are sub-categories for each of the intelligences. The site also provides information about how this view has impacted schools historically and how this theory would affect the implementation of traditional education.

The NC Education Place

http://www.geocities.com/~ educationplace/

This site reviews the basics of learning styles and gives examples of how to use this information in lesson plans. There are guidelines for a well-rounded classroom and techniques for small groups. There are also links to books and classroom resources. In addition, there is a list of schools in North Carolina that have incorporated these ideas and examples of activities and lessons used. Visitors can also view pictures of the students and teachers.

New Dimensions of Learning: Exploring Multiple Intelligences

http://www.multi-intell.com/mi_home.htm

The MI Overview section of this web site allows teachers to click on and explore the eight intelligences. Once linked to an intelligence, teachers will find a list of "core capacities," opportunities to evaluate personal strengths in that area, and a link to lesson ideas (not full plans). These ideas are for a variety of subject areas and are written so as to spark teachers' creativity in lesson planning.

National Reading Styles Institute (NRSI)

http://www.nrsi.com/homepage.html

Founded by Marie Carbo in 1984, NRSI is a research-based educational organization dedicated to improving literacy. NRSI offers teachers and parents help in assisting children who display different reading and learning styles: analytical, global, visual, auditory, tactile, and kinesthetic. The site provides parents and teachers with tools to ensure their children's success in reading and learning by contributing reading tips, quizzes, seminars, conferences, book reviews, and opportunities to ask questions.

Multiple Intelligences Developmental Assessment Scale (MIDAS)

http://www.angelfire.com/oh/themidas/index.html

Named after the testing method used to measure multiple intelligences, MIDAS is an organization created to provide others with awareness of the most proficient way of measuring intelligence. The site provides MIDAS reviews and questions based on the theory of Howard Gardner. As well as offering a MIDAS newsletter, the site recommends material and books, which can be purchased directly through the site, to assist further interest in the mind and intelligence.

Matters of Style: Richard M. Felder

http://www2.ncsu.edu/unity/lockers/users/f/felder/public/Papers/LS-Prism.htm

Felder informs educators that they must "teach around the cycle," to make sure the learning needs of students in each model category are met at least part of the time. The site examines four learning style models (Myers-Briggs Type Indicator, Kolb's Learning Style Model, Herrmann Brain Dominance Instrument, and Felder-Silverman Learning Style Mode) and how they can be applied to students to address both their strengths and weaknesses. Additional readings on these learning style models are also provided.

Learning Styles and Multiple Intelligence: An Explanation of Learning Styles and Multiple Intelligence (MI)

http://www.ldpride.net/learningstyles.MI.htm

This site provides an explanation of learning styles and multiple intelligence. It tells you about the six types of learning styles and how each type of learner best retains information. The site also provides viewers with a list of different types of intelligence. It includes a chat room and links to other sites about learning styles and multiple intelligence. There is also information about different learning disabilities.

It *should be GT world*—Frequently Asked Questions about . . . Testing Our Gifted Children

http://www.gtworld.org/gttest.htm

This web site contains the answers to frequently asked questions (FAQ) about gifted children. The FAQ site defines and describes the different types of tests children are required to take during their educational careers. The main link for this site is GT World, a publisher of books and articles, which are provided as resources for parents. In addition, GT World provides a comprehensive list of web links to reference sites, early entrance college programs, academic programs, mailing lists, and advocacy groups.

Gifted Development Center (GDC)

http://www.gifteddevelopment.com/

This web site is a service provided by the Institute for the Study of Advanced Development. The main focus of GDC is to introduce and describe the concept of visual spatial learning. An exercise is provided to discover if someone is a visual spatial learner. In addition, links are provided to other articles and resource materials pertaining to this type of student.

Learning Styles

http://www.geocities.com/CollegePark/Union/2106/ls.html

Teachers will find an all-inclusive guide to learning styles here and may want to use this site as a starting point for gaining personal understanding. This web site has numerous internal links to introduce teachers to learning style theory, from a thorough explanation of "the basics" to hints on creating classroom rules and recommendations on how to arrange a classroom so as to be compatible with the various learning styles. An extensive reference list is also included.

Additional Multiple Intelligences Sites

Secondary School Educators: Learning Style Assessments Links

http://7-12educators.about.com/cs/learnstyleassess/

Harvard Project Zero

http://pzweb.harvard.edu/

Theatre in Motion

http://www.theatreinmotion.com/

Mrs. Young's Page on Multiple Intelligences

http://www.fortunecity.com/millenium/garston/49/multiintell.html

New Horizons for Learning

http://www.newhorizons.org

ENGLISH FOR SPEAKERS OF OTHER LANGUAGES

By 2020, it is estimated that Hispanics will be the largest ethnic minority group in the United States. For many children, Spanish is the first language learned and continues to be the main language spoken in the home. Additionally, the United States continues to be enriched by immigrants from countries all over the world. Many cities have ethnic enclaves of language minority and immigrant groups. For social studies teachers, it can be a challenge to tailor lessons to meet the needs of students who are English language learners. The following web sites will assist teachers in learning more about the special needs of language minority students and in adapting existing lessons for them.

Bilingual Resources

http://www.eduplace.com/bil/index.html

One of Houghton Mifflin's sites, this is a collection of bibliographies and links to the best and most useful Internet sites for bilingual education teachers. It can be accessed in both Spanish and English.

Welcome-Bienvenidos

Reprinted with permission of Dr. Isabel Schon/California State University.

Barahona Center for the Study of Books in Spanish for Children and Adolescents

http://www.csusm.edu/campus_centers/csb

This site includes a list of recommended books in Spanish, books about Latinos in English, information on workshops and conferences, and hundreds of related links. It can be accessed in both Spanish and English.

Center for Applied Linguistics

http://www.cal.org

Dedicated to "improving communication through better understanding of language and culture," this center's comprehensive site features research, teaching materials, and other resources for ESOL, foreign languages, and linguistics.

Dave's ESL Café

http://www.eslcafe.com

Billed as "The Internet's Meeting Place for ESL/EFL Students and Teachers from Around the World!", this easy-to-navigate site offers many resources for both students and teachers. The Hint of the Day and the Idea Cookbook offer ice breakers, teaching tips, and games.

ESL Lounge

http://www.esl-lounge.com

This excellent teachers' site is loaded with lesson plans, worksheets, teaching tips, printable board games, and reviews of notable ESL books.

ESL Magazine Online

http://www.eslmag.com

This site features abstracts of articles from the print magazine for English as a Second Language (ESL) educators. Helpful ESL/EFL links are included.

ESL/Bilingual/Foreign Language Lesson Plans and Resources

http://www.csun.edu/~ hcedu013/eslindex.html

Created by a teacher educator at California State University, this site provides many helpful links to lesson plans, resources, study abroad opportunities, and educational standards and frameworks.

Kathy Schrock's Guide for Educators: Foreign Languages, ESL, and General Information

http://discoveryschool.com/schrockguide/world/worldrw.html

Links are included to many sites for foreign language and bilingual educators. ESL educators will find several online resources that can be used by both teachers and students.

National Association of Bilingual Education

http://www.nabe.org/

This organization is dedicated to promoting equity for language minority students through bilingual education. The site includes the latest updates regarding legislation and policy, articles about bilingual education, conference information, and links to other sites.

National Clearinghouse for English Language Acquisition

http://www.ncela.gwu.edu

This site offers technical assistance on important issues related to linguistically and culturally diverse students. Users will find links to government and professional sites, an online biweekly news bulletin, journal articles and bibliographies, and state laws and associations.

Teachers of English to Speakers of Other Languages, Inc.

Reprinted with permission of TESOL.

TESOL Connects!

http://www.tesol.org

This is the web site of Teachers of English to Speakers of Other Languages (TESOL). Users can access news, ESL standards for students pre-K through grade 12, grant information, and a "fax on demand" service to have TESOL documents and applications sent to your fax machine 24 hours a day, 7 days a week.

Web Sites Guides for ESL Students

http://www.aitech.ac.jp/~iteslj/guides/index.html

Two web site guides and accompanying exercises give ESL students opportunities to practice English in relevant, practical ways. CuisineNet uses hundreds of menus from real restaurants; Internet Movie Database lists over 180,000 movies.

CULTURAL DIFFERENCES AMONG LEARNERS

As the U.S. classroom becomes increasingly diverse, educators have responded by trying to incorporate and meet the needs and interests of students who reflect a variety of cultures, religions, and languages. Social studies teachers and students will find the following web sites helpful not only for learning more about the beliefs and practices of special populations, but also for learning how to structure and monitor learning and classroom exercises to best meet the needs of diverse cognitive styles.

Welcome to Amigos! Bienvenidos a Amigos!

Reprinted with permission of Carmen Guanipa.

Amigos

http://edweb.sdsu.edu/people/cguanipa/amigos

This multicultural site is intended primarily for middle and high school students and their parents and teachers. It includes essays on diversity issues, information on additional resources, personal stories, and intergenerational experiences. The site can be accessed in both Spanish and English.

Appreciating Differences

http://www.geocities.com/Athens/Parthenon/4904/index.html

This web site is "dedicated to helping teachers, parents, and students appreciate differences." Links such as Disability Awareness, Cultural Awareness, and Multiple Intelligences lead to many educational resources, lesson plans, and other sites.

Awesome Library: Multicultural

http://www.awesomelibrary.org/Classroom/Social_Studies/Multicultural/ Multicultural.html

This site provides links and sources for both multicultural and international issues. Users can access information about specific cultural groups and nationalities, retrieve lesson plans, and find pen pals from diverse backgrounds.

Clearinghouse for Multicultural/Bilingual Education

http://catsis.weber.edu/MBE/HTMLs/MBE.html

The Clearinghouse provides resources, information, and teaching materials for pre-K through post-secondary educators. A comprehensive index facilitates searches. It is an excellent gateway site to periodicals, professional organizations, and teaching aids, such as posters and pictures.

ERIC Digests

http://www.ericfacility.net/ericdigests/index/

This site presents thousands of articles, essays, and teaching ideas on a multitude of education topics, including diversity issues.

Multicultural Pavilion

http://www.edchange.org/multicultural

This online resource provides reviews, links, and awareness activities for teachers, students, and parents. The Teacher's Corner includes strategies for fostering multicultural understanding in the classroom.

Peace Corps Kids World

http://www.peacecorps.gov/kids

Intended for elementary and middle school students, Kids World provides information about the diverse cultures on earth. The site also stresses the importance of service and volunteerism. Students can apply what they have learned in an interactive game.

Standards: The International Journal of Multicultural Studies

http://www.colorado.edu/journals/standards

This full-text journal includes articles, images, reviews, and links to multicultural educational resources on the Internet.

National Association for Multicultural Education (NAME)

http://www.nameorg.org

NAME is an organization of diverse educators and activists from around the world. This site features publications, position papers, links to related journals and magazines, as well as lesson plans and a reference library.

We Hold These Truths to be Self-Evident:
Evidence of Democratic Principles in Our Schools

Part 1: Investigating Special Populations

Reprinted with permission of Carla Mathison.

We Hold These Truths to Be Self-Evident

http://edweb.sdsu.edu/people/cmathison/truths/truths.html

The site guides educators in the exploration of multiculturalism, democratic principles, and special populations in the United States. The Culminating Web Quest Activity can be completed in small groups.

INCLUSION OF STUDENTS WITH DISABILITIES

Some 43,000,000 Americans have one or more physical or mental disabilities, and this number is increasing. In 1990, the Americans with Disabilities Act was passed to alleviate the problem of reduced opportunities for individuals with disabilities and the tendency of society to isolate and segregate these individuals. With the enactment of this law, teachers need additional knowledge and skills to assist their students with disabilities.

Special Education Resources from the Champion International Middle School Partnership

http://www.middleschool.com/administrators/res_specialed.html

From this site, educators can reach other selected gateways that lead to hundreds of important resources. This is a good place for busy teachers and administrators to start.

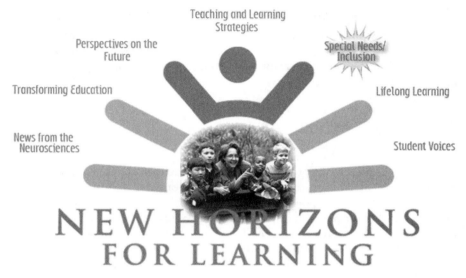

Teaching and Learning
Strategies

Perspectives on the
Future

Special Needs/
Inclusion

Transforming Education

Lifelong Learning

News from the
Neurosciences

Student Voices

NEW HORIZONS
FOR LEARNING

Quarterly Journal   Current Notices

About New Horizons for Learning   Join our Learning Community   Survey/Feedback
Site Index   NHFL Products   WABS   Meeting Spaces   Search

Reprinted with permission of New Horizons for Learning.

Inclusive Schools: Inclusion of Students with Special Needs

http://www.inclusion.org

Provided by Washington's State Superintendent of Public Instruction, "Inclusive Schools: Inclusion of Students with Special Needs" is a database serving all teachers and school districts. It provides information on laws, best practices, examples of programs, and recommended resources for inclusion.

The Inclusion Network

http://www.inclusion.org/

Sponsored by Cincinnati Bell Telephone and Federated Department Stores, this site serves as a gateway for dozens of resources related to education, employment, community inclusion, and advocacy for people with disabilities.

Council for Exceptional Children

http://www.cec.sped.org/

This huge professional organization is the place to start for information and resources about children and young adults with disabilities. This site is a gateway to hundreds of useful and practical resources for teachers, administrators, and parents.

WORKING WITH AT-RISK STUDENTS AND YOUTH

At-Risk students present unique problems and often require school-wide initiatives due to the nature of the socioeconomic causes. The following web sites provide research and information on initiatives and strategies that can be used by teachers as individuals or as school leaders.

Pathways to School Improvement

http://www.ncrel.org/sdrs/areas/at0cont.htm

This high-quality site, provided by the North Central Regional Educational Laboratory (NCREL), is an easy-to-navigate point of entry to gain access to some of the best resources on the Internet for teaching at-risk students. Be sure to check out their Trip Planner Inventory, a special tool designed to help begin the school improvement process. The Trip Planner helps map out where to go within *Pathways* to get the information and resources needed to transform local schools.

National Institute on the Education of At-Risk Students

http://www.ed.gov/offices/OERI/At-Risk/

The At-Risk Institute supports a range of research and development activities designed to improve the education of students at risk of educational failure because of limited English proficiency, poverty, race, geographic location, or economic disadvantage.

Laboratory for Student Success (LSS)

http://www.temple.edu/LSS/

LSS is a federally funded activity located at the Mid-Atlantic Regional Educational Laboratory at Temple University. It is designed to help schools launch reform initiatives that promote school success for at-risk youth. High academic achievement in urban schools is its focus.

National Dropout Prevention Center

http://www.dropoutprevention.org/

This site features research, publications, and information on the best practices that are designed to keep kids in school until they earn a high school diploma. This easy-to-use site leads educators to exceptional resources.

Urban Education Web

http://eric-web.tc.columbia.edu

"Dedicated to urban students, their families, and the educators who serve them," this site offers exceptional information about working with at-risk students, but also includes resources on many other issues affecting the success of urban youth.

Council of Great City Schools

http://www.cgcs.org

This "organization of the nation's largest urban public school systems, advocating K–12 education in inner-city schools," takes on the most challenging of educational issues in this nation's most daunting settings. Its web site provides excellent resources for those who share its mission and goals.

Middle Web

http://www.middleweb.com

A service of the Edna McConnell Clark Foundation, Middle Web is a comprehensive resource for information, news, and tips on the best practices to promote success for middle school youngsters from all walks of life. This award-winning site offers stories of real teachers and real schools struggling with the challenge of standards-based reform.

FAMILY INVOLVEMENT IN EDUCATION

Family involvement in education is a critical variable in school success, which can be expanded with help from the information contained on these web sites.

About.com

http://home.about.com/home

About.com is one of the most comprehensive resource sites on the Internet. Use it as a gateway to search for help on virtually any topic. From the Home and Family page, scroll down to their section on Parenting. It includes information on school success, parenting strategies for children and adolescents, help for parents of special needs children, advice for single parents and stepparents, and a host of other critical topics for parents and educators. For teachers, this is an excellent place to find information to give to parents who are helping their children overcome specific problems and challenges.

Champion Middle School Partnership

http://www.middleschool.com/studentbehavior/sb_conference.html

Champion International Corporation's Middle School Partnership web site provides a rich assortment of resources to promote parent participation in the education of contemporary students. Especially useful is the information for both parents and teachers on how to prepare for effective conferences, even when they involve contentious issues. The site also provides links to more comprehensive parenting aids, including the popular "Help Your Child" series from the U.S. Department of Education and parent networks that provide information on everything from children's health to school success.

Children, Youth and Family Consortium

http://www.cyfc.umn.edu/

The Children, Youth and Family Consortium at the University of Minnesota provides both parents and educators with excellent resources and links that help parents participate meaningfully in the education of their children. This site is particularly well-equipped with resources supporting stepfamilies and children of divorce. It also houses parent support groups and links to interactive sites that allow parents to seek advice and counsel from other parents and from youth-serving professionals.

National Parent Information Network

http://www.npin.org

The National Parent Information Network, sponsored by ERIC, the U.S. Department of Education's information resource, provides a comprehensive library of publications about parenting, parent involvement in school, and successful child-raising practices. Most of the material is in full-text versions and can be downloaded or printed on a home or school computer. The publications on this site cover behavior and discipline, school performance, and coping with high-risk behavior. It is one of the most comprehensive and authoritative resources available for educators and families.

Family Education

http://www.familyeducation.com/home/

FamilyEducation.com is an engaging, interactive information center for parents of K–12 students. It includes articles, tips and advice, discussions, downloads, and a chance to ask the experts for help and support. Confronting challenging topics, this site handles delicate issues with solid advice and dignity.

United States Department of Education

http://www.ed.gov/pubs/parents

The U.S. Department of Education provides free, high-quality materials that help promote parent involvement in their children's education. Some of the most useful publications come from the "Helping Your Child" series—a collection of publications designed to help parents foster healthy development, productive behavior, and success in school. The "Family Involvement in Education" publications focus on building productive collaborations among the school, the home, and the community to improve schools and boost student achievement. Publications devoted to "Learning Activities" and "Reading Improvement" give parents specific ways of helping their child extend school learning.

National Parent Teachers Association

http://www.pta.org

The web site of the National PTA not only keeps parents up-to-date on the activities of the association, but also provides links to hundreds of child-advocacy groups around the world. If schools are looking for guidance on family-friendly programs and parent involvement, this is the place to begin.

Partnership for Family Involvement in Education

http://pfie.ed.gov/

This government program is designed to increase opportunities for families to be more involved in their children's learning at school and at home and to use family-school-community partnerships to strengthen schools and improve student achievement.

CHAPTER 12

Planning and Instruction

Lesson plans are the vehicles by which teachers deliver information for students to learn. The best lesson plans are well prepared, standards-based, and educationally sound; they are also creative and interesting and promote active learning. The technology available today allows teachers to reach beyond what has been done in the past and enhance instruction.

LESSON PLANNING TO MEET STANDARDS AND BENCHMARKS

The Internet provides a venue for teachers to borrow ideas and adapt them for their own lessons, connect with other teachers and classrooms, and facilitate and expand their own and their students' learning.

The collection of web sites found below is but a small sampling of the hundreds of sites for teachers. These exceptional sites were chosen based on the following criteria: They are easy to understand and navigate, most offer access to state or national curriculum standards, they provide teachers with free lesson plans and teaching resources, most have resources for all grade levels, and many offer information for a number of academic subjects and include interdisciplinary ideas.

Creating lesson plans that are linked to state or national curriculum standards is vital to promoting an effective educational environment. As teachers explore these web sites, they are encouraged to investigate those that include information on standards, benchmarks, and frameworks and, in turn, to incorporate these standards into the lessons they teach.

Marco Polo

http://www.marcopolo-education.org/index.aspx

This excellent site offers links to seven other web sites: ArtsEdge (for arts education), EconLink (for economics education), EdSitement (for humanities education), Illuminations (for mathematics education), Read-Write-Think (for English), Science Netlinks (for science education), and Xpeditions (for geography education). Each of these sites is sponsored, and some were created, by well-known and respected educational organizations. Provided within each site are lesson plans for K–12 education that are standards-based.

Teacher Explorer Center

http://ss.uno.edu/SS/homePages/SSLib.html

The Teacher Explorer Center is appropriately named. Created by the University of New Orleans, the center's home page offers 40 links under the following five categories: content resources, lesson plans, teaching with technology, teacher resources, and research theory. Each of these links provides even more site listings, often with brief descriptions.

The New York Times Learning Network

http://www.nytimes.com/learning

The New York Times offers this excellent web site for teachers to use in the classroom. There are current news items (written in summary), but this site will take students beyond just what they read. Teachers can link to hundreds of lesson plans for current and past events—there is a lesson plan archive—and are provided with ideas for interdisciplinary lessons as well. All lessons are standards-based, and the site offers links to information on standards. A daily current events quiz and links for parents and students are also included.

Reprinted with permission of Karla Mickey.

Education World

http://www.education-world.com

This web site might be described as the one-stop shopping place for teachers. The number of resources is astounding. Educators will find articles and lesson plans as well as links to other sites and international research. For teachers who are unsure of what they hope to find on the Internet, Education World is a good place to start looking—but one should allow plenty of time for all the exploring opportunities available here.

McREL

http://www.mcrel.com/resources/index.asp

This web site is a part of McREL (Mid-continent Regional Education Laboratory). Standards and benchmarks are the main focus. Lesson plans on this site are listed by subject, and within each topic is a Related Content Standard link that details the standard associated with the lesson plan. Each standard is also described as primary, upper elementary, middle school/junior high, or high school and can then be linked to a corresponding benchmark. Connections+ is excellent for teachers who need help in relating and citing standards and benchmarks in their lessons.

Reprinted with permission of Margaret A. Hill, Ph.D.

SCORE History/Social Science Online Resources

http://score.rims.k12.ca.us

SCORE (Schools of California Online Resources for Educators) is an excellent web site that provides educators with links to numerous resources and lesson plans. Also included on this site is a link to California's frameworks, standards, and assessments. SCORE has two other links on its home page for Teacher Talk and Internet Classrooms, allowing for opportunities for teachers and students to contact other teachers and classrooms.

ePALS Classroom Exchange

http://www.epals.com/index.html

While the ePALS web site does not provide direct access to lesson plans, teachers will be encouraged to learn and share educational experiences and projects through the classroom exchange. This site boasts an e-mail membership of over 15,000 classrooms in 107 countries. One can search for classrooms in a country and be presented with a short introduction from each participating teacher, who will include information on class size, grade level, and purpose for joining. Dozens of other web site resources are also included that will link teachers to recommended educational sites.

Reprinted with permission of Cable in the Classroom CCI/Crosby Publishing.

Cable in the Classroom

http://www.ciconline.org/home.htm

Cable in the Classroom is an initiative by the cable industry through which schools receive free cable service, including more than 540 hours per month of commercial-free educational programming. Highlights of the Cable in the Classroom web site include Search the Listings, Curriculum Connections, and Professional Development Institute/Virtual Workshops. Search the Listings allows teachers to enter keywords or subjects and get lists of relevant curriculum-based programs airing with extended copyright clearances on 40 cable networks. Most networks have study guides and lesson plans available via the Internet; CICOnline also has links to all the network sites. Curriculum Connections focuses on how selected programs can be used to help students meet curriculum standards. Within the Professional Development Institute section, teachers can take virtual workshops, find links to top educational web sites, and find the locations of upcoming hands-on workshops.

 Center for Civic Education

Reprinted with permission of Center for Civic Education.

Center for Civic Education

http://civiced.org/lesson-plans.html

Although there are currently only 13 lesson plans provided on this page within the web site, the lessons are quite detailed and expect students to think critically as they read and discuss issues in civics education. All but one of the lessons have two links: One provides text and questions for students, and the other provides the teacher's guide.

The Copernicus Education Gateway

http://www.gocopernicus.com

Updated continuously and full of a wide variety of interesting information and links to some great educational resources, Go Copernicus is an excellent web site and a recommended starting point for teachers searching for lesson plans, many of which are linked to standards. Teachers will want to allow plenty of time to explore this site and all it has to offer.

Reprinted with permission of Charles Hill.

Developing Educational Standards

http://edstandards.org/Standards.html

Putnam Valley and Wappingers Central School districts in New York have created a web site dedicated to providing access to the educational standards of 15 subjects, all 50 states, the U.S. government, and a few other nations. In addition, educators will find extensive resource listings under easy to use categories, such as Centers, Clearinghouses, and Labs; State-Focused Groups; Other Organizations; and Newspapers and Magazines. While there are no lesson plans here, this site will be quite useful to teachers creating standards-based lessons.

Reprinted with permission of ERIC Clearinghouse for Social Studies/Social Science Education at Indiana University.

ERIC Clearinghouse for Social Studies/Social Science Education (ERIC/Chess)

http://www.indiana.edu/~ssdc/eric_chess.htm

ERIC/Chess is an online clearinghouse that specializes in providing social science educators with updated information and resources on published materials on teaching and learning. This site contains many services for teachers, parents, students, administrators, and researchers who are interested in using the ERIC database as a resource for their areas of interest. ERIC/CHESS provides visitors with a service that will answer questions about using the ERIC database, a reproduction service for ERIC documents, newsletters on topics in education, and full texts of *ERIC Digest*. This site contains helpful information on how to submit documents to ERIC, how to obtain documents from ERIC, and how to search on the ERIC database. It also allows easy access to curriculum and teaching guides, lesson plans, workshops, descriptions of upcoming conferences, and lists of support services for social science educators. ERIC/Chess provides a comprehensive list of the best links to other Internet sites that are excellent resources for social studies, education, history, art, and other related areas. Educators can also find a list of all the social studies standards and benchmarks for each of the 50 states.

Additional Planning Web Sites

The Learning Site

http://www.harcourtschool.com

Awesome Library

http://www.awesomelibrary.org

Exploring Ancient World Cultures

http://eawc.evansville.edu

LDOnline: Learning Disabilities Information

http://www.ldonline.org

Mr. Donn's Ancient History

http://members.aol.com/donnandlee/index.html

New Horizons for Learning

http://www.newhorizons.org

The Odyssey

http://www.worldtrek.org/odyssey/teachers/index.html

A to Z Teacher Stuff

http://AtoZTeacherStuff.com

The ACCESS INDIANA Teaching and Learning Center

http://www.k12tlc.net

Ask Asia

http://www.askasia.org/for_educators/fe_frame.htm

AskERIC Lesson Plans

http://ericir.syr.edu/Virtual/Lessons

Busy Teacher's Web Site K–12

http://www.ceismc.gatech.edu/busyt

Encarta

http://encarta.msn.com/schoolhouse

Kathy Schrock's Guide for Educators

http://discoveryschool.com/schrockguide

Odin's Castle

http://www.odinscastle.org

Kathy Schrock's Guide for Educators: WebQuests in Our Future

http://discoveryschool.com/schrockguide/webquest/webquest.html

Ozlines: WebQuests for Learning

http://www.ozline.com/webquests

The WebQuest Page

http://edweb.sdsu.edu/webquest/webquest.html

WebQuests and Resources for Teachers

http://www.davison.k12.mi.us/academic/hewitt14.htm

ASSESSMENT AND HIGH-STAKES TESTING

The trend toward statewide testing as a measure of the success of students, teachers, and schools has presented additional considerations for teachers as they develop their goals and teaching strategies. This section provides information on assessment and standards.

Content Knowledge: The McREL Standards Data Base

http://www.mcrel.org/standards-benchmarks/index.asp

Described by the authors as "a compendium of standards and benchmarks for K–12 education," this site is an excellent place to start in planning standards-based instruction at the local level. Included are instructional activities that are linked to specific national and state standards. This site is an excellent tool for teachers interested in promoting strong test performance among students.

Fair Test

http://fairtest.org

Fair Test is a national, nonprofit organization devoted to preventing abuses and misuses of standardized testing and to assuring that student evaluation is accurate, sound, and unbiased. This is an excellent gateway to both Fair Test materials and other sites advocating for assessment reform.

U.S. Department of Education

http://www.ed.gov/index.jsp

Go to the DOE web site, click on "Accountability," and you will find a long list of assessment and evaluation resources from this U.S. department and the various labs and centers it supports.

ERIC Clearinghouse on Assessment and Evaluation

http://www.askeric.org

This clearinghouse provides excellent resources on best practices, the fair use of assessment data, and balanced information on high-stakes testing.

High Stakes: Testing for Tracking, Promotion, and Graduation

http://www.nap.edu/readingroom/books/highstakes

This very thoughtful and carefully researched document lays out the major issues in high-stakes testing and its use for promotion, graduation, placement, and tracking. This is an excellent scholarly work.

HOMEWORK HELPER

The Internet offers the opportunity for students to access information at home so that they can progress through assignments when the teacher is not available. In addition, many students derive benefits from practice and enriching exercises. The following sites can be used at home or at school for students to work individually or in groups.

Reprinted with permission of Study Web.

Study Web

http://www.lightspan.com

This web site is a gateway to a comprehensive set of tools in Study Buddy and search engines for content information for students working on homework assignments.

Homework Central

http://www.homeworkcentral.com

Neatly organized by subject areas, this site offers a variety of content resources and tools. Students will benefit from accessing the study games and test preparation. Teachers will also appreciate the over 14,000 searchable lesson plans that are available.

Kids on the Web

http://www.zen.org/~brendan/kids.html

In addition to offering a Homework Tools section of encyclopedias and other reference works, the Fun Stuff sections offer opportunities for independent learning.

CEO Express

http:/www.ceoexpress.com

Designed to give busy executives easy access to web site resources, its volume of current events and economic information makes it valuable for students. This site is particularly useful for social studies report writing and project preparation.

Britannica.com

http://www.britannica.com

This all-purpose site offers links, organized by social studies content areas, to some of the best information online. In addition to accessing the complete encyclopedia, students can link to other web sites, magazines, and related books.

Encarta.com

http://encarta.msn.com/

The Encarta web site is an online encyclopedia that can be searched for specific information on most topics in social studies.

Homework Made Simple

http://www.homemadesimple.com/

Home Made Simple makes homework easy. You'll find an amazing collection of education resources with puzzles, mazes, quizzes, and other interactive ways to learn.

Teachers' Tool Kit

Professional growth and development are crucial to a teacher's success. Social studies teachers have a variety of tools on the Internet to enhance their instruction and professional growth. Three of the most useful are professional organizations; electronic journals, electronic newspapers, and news sources; and sites on classroom management.

PROFESSIONAL ORGANIZATIONS

In addition to the National Council for the Social Studies, social studies teachers have a number of professional organizations that provide guidance, support, and materials for the teaching of the content area. In many cases, membership is not even required to access the excellent resources available for educators and students. Some of the best are listed here in alphabetical order.

American Anthropological Association

http://www.aaanet.org

Provides an overview of what anthropology is, free access to several publications, and links to anthropology resources on the Internet.

American Council of Learned Societies (ACLS)

http://www.acls.org

The ACLS is a federation of 61 scholarly organizations related to the social sciences. Education-related projects include a K–12 program designed to improve humanities education in the schools. Also included is information on teacher exchanges with other countries.

American Educational Research Association

http://www.aera.net

This network features online resources, such as educational reports, abstracts archives for three professional journals, and news and jobs postings. Information about other Internet resources is also provided.

American Forum for Global Education (AFGE)

http://www.globaled.org

The AFGE promotes "the education of our nation's youth for responsible citizenship in an increasingly interconnected and rapidly changing world." The site also allows an exchange of ideas and provides instructional materials and professional development opportunities for teachers and administrators.

American Geographical Society

http://www.amergeog.org

In addition to information about the organization and its membership, this site includes abstracts and images from *The Geographical Review,* geographic photo displays, and 3D virtual tours.

American Historical Association

http://www.theaha.org

Billed as the professional association for all historians, this organization has a K–12 teaching specialization and offers joint membership with other related organizations. Links to other sites are also provided.

American Political Science Association (APSA)

http://www.apsanet.org

The APSA is the world's largest organization for the study of political life. Membership benefits include two quarterly publications, interdisciplinary affiliations, and free electronic notification of research news and Washington, D.C., alerts.

American Psychological Association

http://www.apa.org

The national organization for psychologists and mental health professionals also offers comprehensive information for educators, parents, and teens. Students can access information about career planning, education programs, and college summer programs.

American Psychological Society (APS)

http://www.psychologicalscience.org

The APS's Teaching Resources section offers an excellent overview of the research and application of the field. All major subdisciplines are included as well as exemplary syllabi and PowerPoint presentations.

American Sociological Association (ASA)

http://www.asanet.org

For high school teachers, this site has several useful features in addition to general membership information. It has a K–12 collaborative program with information on the Advanced Placement Examination as well as an excellent Teaching Resources Center for high school teachers, which includes syllabi, primers, videos, and other instructional materials. Students can access the ASA Resources for Students section, which discusses honors programs, research support, and careers in sociology.

American Studies Association (ASA)

http://www.georgetown.edu/crossroads/asainfo.html

The ASA promotes the study of past and present American culture. The online newsletter provides full-text curriculum articles for teachers and administrators.

Association for Supervision and Curriculum Development (ASCD)

http://www.ascd.org

The ASCD's emphasis is on K–12 educational leadership and curriculum. The site includes articles and news stories on timely topics, samples from *Educational Leadership*, and information on professional development.

Reprinted with permission of the Association of American Geographers.

Association of American Geographers (AAG)

http://www.aag.org

The AAG is an educational and scientific society that provides publications and resources for the teaching of geography. The site features hands-on learning activities and readings in world and U.S. geography. Links to related organizations and sites provide further resources and materials.

Geographic Education National Implementation Project

http://genip.tamu.edu/right.htm

This consortium of professional geography associations seeks to improve education in the discipline. Links to other organizations and ideas for staff development are included. A biannual newsletter can also be accessed from the site.

Reprinted with permission of Global TeachNet, National Peace Corps Association.

Global TeachNet

http://www.1wow.org/pages/teach.html

This network, organized by the National Peace Corps Association, seeks to bring global perspectives to U.S. classrooms by disseminating global education materials and resources to K–12 teachers.

National Association for Humanities Education (NAHE)

http://www.nahe.org

This professional organization of teachers and scholars in the humanities also includes museum directors and other interested individuals. Links to museums, libraries, and Internet resources are provided as well as information about its journal and newsletter.

National Association for Multicultural Education (NAME)

http://www.nameorg.org

NAME is composed of a diverse group of educators and activists from around the world. It publishes position papers, a professional journal, and lesson plans, all related to issues of diversity.

National Association of Economic Educators (NAEE)

http://ecedweb.unomaha.edu/naee/naeepamp.htm

The NAEE seeks to encourage and support objective economic education programs at all levels. It serves as a dissemination organ by which ideas, lessons, and effective practices are exchanged among educators.

National Council for Geographic Education (NCGE)

http://www.ncge.org

The NCGE offers publications, geography resources, and links to other sites. Information about upcoming activities, annual meetings, and award programs is also provided.

National Council for the Social Studies (NCSS)

http://www.ncss.org

The NCSS is the nation's largest and oldest professional organization devoted to social studies education. On this site, teachers can find national curriculum standards, journals and publications, and teaching resources.

National Council on Economic Education (NCEE)

http://www.nationalcouncil.org/news/index.html

The organization which has official standards and guidelines for economic education. The site provides the latest news in the field, online lessons, and links to other helpful sites.

National Education Association (NEA)

http://www.nea.org

The NEA is the nation's largest association of professional educators. Its web site has been nationally recognized for being informative and user-friendly. Included in this comprehensive site are the NEA Code of Ethics, school district statistics, links to educational policy sites, online multimedia teaching resources, and many other articles and materials of use to classroom teachers.

National Geographic Society (NGS)

http://www.nationalgeographic.com

The familiar yellow-bordered magazine is just one of the many resources available through the NGS. Of particular interest to educators are the Geography Education, Info Central, and World Magazine for Kids features.

National Middle School Association (NMSA)

http://www.nmsa.org

The NMSA is an organization for middle-school-level educators and administrators. This web site offers discussion of timely topics and controversies, K–12 teacher resources, and links to libraries and museums, among other services.

Organization of American Historians

http://www.indiana.edu/~oah

This organization, devoted to the study of American history, offers precollegiate teaching units written by teams of teachers and historians using primary documents. It also offers links to other associations related to history and its teaching.

Reprinted with permission of Phi Delta Kappa International.

Phi Delta Kappa (PDK)

http://www.pdkintl.org

PDK is an international organization of professional educators with an emphasis on public schools. This site provides summaries of educational research, information on travel and professional development, and partial access to articles in *Kappan Magazine*.

World History Association (WHA)

http://www.woodrow.org/teachers/world-history

In partnership with the Woodrow Wilson Leadership Program for Teachers, the WHA hosts an annual meeting, publishes conference papers, and provides teaching materials and modules on its web site.

ELECTRONIC JOURNALS

Keeping abreast of new teaching techniques and curriculum issues can be a daunting prospect for classroom teachers. Fortunately, the World Wide Web is now home to a variety of professional journals that can keep us informed about current practices and controversies. The following journals permit either full or partial access to contents free of charge. In some cases, a modest subscription fee is required for full access to all features.

American Diplomacy

http://www.unc.edu/depts/diplomat

This electronic journal features free subscription to the quarterly publication. Articles include commentary and analysis on American foreign policy. The archive allows users to access past articles, reviews, and related web sites.

American Quarterly

http://crossroads.georgetown.edu/aq/alphsub.html

American Quarterly is an interdisciplinary journal for the study and teaching of American culture. Nonmembers can access full-text articles by browsing the site's archive.

Anthropology and Education Quarterly

http://www.aaanet.org/cae/aeq/index.htm

This journal publishes scholarship on schooling in social and cultural contexts, on human learning both inside and outside of schools, and on the teaching of anthropology. The web site provides a table of contents and abstracts of current and past issues.

APA Monitor

http://www.apa.org/monitor

Full-text access to the American Psychological Association's online newsletter. The Education feature includes articles for psychology teachers of all levels as well as model school programs and fairs.

Bryn Mawr Classical Review and The Medieval Review

http://ccat.sas.upenn.edu/bmcr/subform.html

Free subscription to two electronic journals published by Bryn Mawr College. The first features reviews of current scholarly works in the field of classical studies. The second offers reviews of current work in all areas of medieval studies. Both have searchable archives.

CSS Journal: Computers in the Social Sciences

http://www.webcom.com/journal

Computers in the Social Studies focuses on promoting computers and related technology in social studies classrooms at all education levels. In addition to provocative articles, the site has a searchable archive, provides links to other social studies sites, and has sample historical documents.

Reprinted with permission of Earthworks.

Earthworks

http://www.utexas.edu/depts/grg/eworks/eworks.html

This refereed journal focusing on contemporary geographic issues offers full access to its contents. The Web in Education feature is especially useful for teachers.

Education Week

http://www.edweek.org

This online newspaper for educators includes news items, commentaries, and special reports. A searchable archive and States Pages make this site useful for retrieving specific information quickly. The enormously helpful *Teacher Magazine* can also be accessed from here.

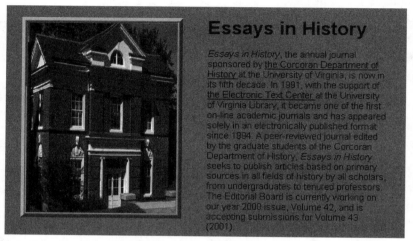

Reprinted with permission of Essays in History, a journal of Corcoran Department of History at UVA.

Essays in History

http://etext.virginia.edu/journals/EH

An annual publication by graduate history students at the University of Virginia, this electronic journal offers full-text articles that span all fields of history. Past issues (from 1990) are also available.

Foreign Affairs Magazine

http://www.foreignaffairs.org

The Weekly Column features excellent analyses of international developments. Related web sites include links to world news, commentary, multicultural resources, and regional studies.

Internet Archaeology

http://intarch.york.ac.uk

Registration to access the full text of articles is required, but free. Teachers of anthropology and history will benefit from the scholarly articles and discussions.

Journal of Economic Education

http://www.indiana.edu/~econed/index.html

Content and pedagogy are both addressed in this electronic journal, which features innovative articles on a variety of cutting-edge teaching media.

National Review Online

http://www.nationalreview.com

Although only partial contents are available on this site, it is nonetheless a useful resource for obtaining conservative perspectives on political issues. Websclusives offers several features available only on the web site.

Perspectives Online

http://www.theaha.org/perspectives

The electronic newsletter of the American Historical Association features full access to scholarly articles on historical topics as well as innovative strategies for teaching history.

Phi Delta Kappan (PDK)

http://www.pdkintl.org/kappan/kappan.htm

Full-text articles are available on a variety of education-related topics. The results of the annual PDK/Gallup Poll of the public's attitudes toward the public schools can be found here.

Political Science Quarterly

http://www.psqonline.org

This electronic journal offers a partial sampling of full-text articles and reviews. Civics and government teachers can read insightful analyses of current political issues and events.

PS Online

http://www.apsanet.org/PS

PS Online is the American Political Science Association's online version of *Political Science and Politics*. The Teaching feature includes guidelines for K–12 teachers of civics and government as well as a forum to exchange teaching ideas with colleagues.

Scholastic

http://teacher.scholastic.com/index.htm

The online version of the popular school magazine offers a number of classroom-tested resources, ideas, and reproducibles. Students will enjoy completing the online social studies activities and tours.

Teacher Magazine

http://www.teachermagazine.org

It includes discussion of contemporary educational issues, practical teaching advice and solutions, recommended books for teachers and students, summaries of research, and commentaries on a wide variety of topics.

Teaching Sociology

http://www.lemoyne.edu/ts/tsmain.html

Although a subscription is necessary to fully access articles, the table of contents for each issue is provided on the web site, making it a useful tool for finding specific articles.

Reprinted with permission of Yale Political Quarterly.

Yale Political Quarterly

http://www.yale.edu/ypq

Published by Yale undergraduates, this site has several useful features for educators: full-text articles, a compilation of political quotes, political links, and access to back issues.

ELECTRONIC NEWSPAPERS AND NEWS SOURCES

The hallmark of the social studies has always been staying abreast of current events. The Internet, with its immediate coverage of worldwide events and issues, is a powerful resource for teachers and students. Several newspapers, magazines, and news services allow us to obtain up-to-the-minute information, analyses, and visuals of breaking stories. Many sites also offer entertaining news quizzes to test understanding.

American Journalism Review Newslink

http://newslink.org/

It offers thousands of links to newspapers, magazines, and news services worldwide and also includes articles on journalism.

Ultimate Collection of News Links

http://pppp.net/links/news/report.html

Over 10,000 links to newspapers and magazines from around the world are provided on this site.

The New York Times Learning Network

http://www.nytimes.com/learning

In addition to providing up-to-the-minute information on current events, the Learning Network links users to additional news and education resources on the World Wide Web. Its strength lies in the considerable archives of its host, *The New York Times*. Teachers will find the daily lesson plans—with thematic connections across the curriculum—very useful. Students will like the interactive news quizzes and the opportunity to send questions to *Times* reporters.

News Directory

http://www.ecola.com/news/press

This comprehensive site provides links to hundreds of daily and nondaily newspapers in the United States as well as worldwide. Other news sources included are magazines and television.

Awesome Library: Reference and Periodicals

http://www.awesomelibrary.org

The Reference and Periodicals feature on this site allows users to search for news and current events by Subjects, Cities, Countries, USA, and World. By selecting Current Events, visitors are taken to a gateway page that includes lessons, online news sources for all grade levels, and virtual field trips.

Time for Kids

http://www.timeforkids.com

An online version of the print magazine. Elementary students can select from the "grades 2–3" and "grades 4–6" renditions. The site contains current events in both text and multimedia formats. Users can also research past events via a searchable archive.

CNN Interactive

http://www.cnn.com

The cable network's home page includes up-to-the-minute news coverage on a variety of topics. Because it is based on the television show, nearly all of the stories are accompanied by an image or map. Users can also listen to stories in RealAudio, view video clips, and search the archives.

Reprinted with permission of KidNews.

KidNews

http://www.kidnews.com

Linking students and teachers from around the world, this site encourages students to write and submit news stories on a variety of topics. Teachers can also use the Adults Talk feature to exchange teaching ideas and lesson plans.

Newsday Project

http://www.gsn.org/project/newsday

Students cannot only learn about national and international news and issues on this site, but also create their own newspapers. Opportunities exist for students to gather and write news stories, edit articles, create layouts and graphics, and publish the finished product. A link on the site, *Middlezine,* is an electronic magazine created by eighth graders covering an array of topics, such as literature, art, sports, and science.

I'm a Kid

http://www.weeklyreader.com

Coverage of current events can be accessed on a number of grade levels: Pre-K, 1, 2, 3, 4, 5, 6, and Teen. Options for teachers and parents are also available.

Current Events in the Social Studies Classroom

http://www.eduplace.com/ss/current/index.html

It provides a monthly highlight of an issue in the news. Each discussion ends with thought-provoking questions suitable for classroom use. The entertaining Current Events Challenge is divided into Grades 1–3, Grades 4 and Up, and For Teachers.

Learning Resources

http://literacynet.org/cnnsf

Using interactive learning activities, this site seeks to improve literacy and understanding of current events by providing news stories that are easier to understand than standard newspaper articles. In addition to reading the text, students can listen and/or view a video clip. The Instructor Page offers teachers lesson plans and ideas for individualized learning.

Nettizen

http://www.nettizen.com/newspaper/

Online newspaper directory, organized by region and featuring headlines and articles from around the world. Photos, maps, and political cartoons can also be accessed.

Online NewsHour

http://www.pbs.org/newshour

The web site of the popular television news show with Jim Lehrer offers transcripts of current broadcasts (some segments are available in RealAudio). Also included are background briefings, a discussion forum, and an archive, among other features. Of particular note for students is the News for Students section.

U.S. Newspaper Links

http://www.usnpl.com/

This web site provides links to newspapers and TV stations throughout the United States.

Additional Teachers' Tool Kit Web Sites

American Memory: Places in the News

http://memory.loc.gov/ammem/gmdhtml/plnews.html

BBC News

http://news.bbc.co.uk

Children's Express

http://www.childrens-express.org

Kathy Schrock's Guide for Educators: News Sources & Newspapers

http://discoveryschool.com/schrockguide/news/nsp.html

The New York Times on the Web

http://www.nytimes.com

Oneworld.net

http://www.oneworld.org/themes/country/front.shtml

Online Newspapers

http://www.onlinenewspapers.com

Time.com

http://cgi.pathfinder.com/time

Topics Online

http://www.topicsmag.com

CLASSROOM MANAGEMENT

Very few professions ask 22-year-olds to manage 150 people a day to the successful completion of a task. Without classroom management, social studies cannot be taught. Even experienced teachers find significant new challenges that test their ability to manage students and the learning process. The following sites offer some ideas on classroom management strategies.

Works4Me

http://www.nea.org/helpfrom/growing/works4me/library.html

This NEA site offers suggestions on classroom management as well as school climate and instructional planning. Users can link to searchable libraries, forums, and resource units.

You Can Handle Them All

http://www.disciplinehelp.com/default.htm

The web site offers background information on psychological dispositions associated with misbehavior. A very useful tool for diagnosing behaviors is found in the Solutions for Handling 117 Misbehaviors section.

Big Chalk: Classroom Management

http://www.bigchalk.com/cgi-bin/WebObjects/WOPortal.woa/db/Home.html

By submitting "classroom management" to this web site's search engine, teachers can access a number of ideas, primarily in the form of articles from practicing teachers and journals on classroom management.

The Honor Level System

http://www.honorlevel.com/HLS_INTRO.HTML

This site offers a description of an "Honor Level System" and tips on classroom management. Originally developed at the middle school level, it is now used at all grade levels in many U.S. schools.

Teacher Vision

http://www.teachervision.com/lesson-plans/lesson-6429.html

Teacher Vision offers behavior management tips and classroom organization strategies from experienced teachers.

Eric Online Documents

http://searcheric.org/

ERIC has two extensive documents on classroom management here. *Positive Classroom Management: A Step-by-Step Guide,* ED433334, is a 134-page guide to classroom management, and *The First Six Weeks of School,* ED442770, provides information on practices as well as activities to insure the first six weeks gets off to a good start.

About the Authors

Michael J. Berson is an Associate Professor of Social Science Education at the University of South Florida. He is a member of the Social Science Education Consortium, an invitation-only, international group of recognized scholars in social studies. He serves as a board member of the College and University Faculty Assembly of the National Council for the Social Studies (NCSS) and on the Technology Committee. He received the University of South Florida Outstanding Undergraduate Teaching Award and the NCSS President's Award for outstanding contribution to the field. He is a co-founder of the American Educational Research Association SIG Research in Global Child Advocacy and is a member of UNESCO's Innocence in Danger North American National Action Committee on Internet Safety. He has published and presented extensively, focusing his research on global child advocacy and technology in social studies education.

Bárbara C. Cruz is an Associate Professor of Social Science Education at the University of South Florida. Her research interests include global and multicultural perspectives in education, with an emphasis on ethnic minority students. Other interests include innovative teacher preparation practices, active learning strategies, and textbook bias. In addition to academic publications, she is the author of several African-American and Hispanic biographies and young adult books on educational issues such as school dress codes, single sex education, and school violence.

James A. Duplass is a Professor of Social Science Education at the University of South Florida. He is a graduate of Loyola and Saint Louis universities. His publications include *Crescent City Short Stories,* a collection of southern ethnology themes, and academic articles on values education, curriculum design, and thinking skills. He is the past editor of *Trends and Issues,* the journal of the Florida Council for the Social Studies, and has received over $1 million in technology grants. Professor Duplass has recently published, *Teaching Elementary Social Studies: What Every School Teacher Should Know!* (Houghton Mifflin).

J. Howard Johnston is Professor of Secondary Education at the University of South Florida. He has authored over 100 works on middle-level education and has presented over 1,500 invited papers, lectures, and keynote addresses in all 50 U.S. states, 7 Canadian provinces, and more than a dozen countries in Europe, South America, Asia, and the Caribbean. In addition to nine books, he has published in the *NASSP Bulletin, Middle School Journal, Phi Delta Kappan, School Administrator, Schools in the Middle,*

School Boards Journal, and numerous other outlets. He is the recipient of the National Association of Secondary School Principals' Distinguished Service Award, National Middle School Association's Presidential Award for Excellence, and Gruhn-Long Award for lifetime service to middle-level education. He has served on the Board of Trustees of the National Middle School Association and the Council on Middle Level Education for the National Association of Secondary School Principals. He currently serves as a Lead Team consultant for the Champion International Corporation's Middle School Partnership.